THE MENTOR
ESQ
Handbook Series

SUCCESSFUL TRIAL SKILLS

A GUIDE TO JURY SELECTION, OPENING STATEMENTS, DIRECT & CROSS-EXAMINATIONS, AND CLOSING ARGUMENTS

TABLE OF CONTENTS

PREFACE

I am a second-generation trial lawyer. My father and partner, Guy I. Smiley, was actively trying cases at the time he founded our law firm in 1968. I spent most of my high-school, college, and law school years observing my father, and fellow trial lawyers of his generation, in a courtroom. By the time I graduated from Brooklyn Law School in 1996, I had already observed dozens of trials and had actively coached and participated in my law school's Moot Court Program where I oversaw our national trial advocacy teams. I tried – and won – my first trial shortly after becoming admitted to the Bar in January 1997. Since then, I have been continuously trying personal injury cases and I have learned quite a lot about how to have success in a courtroom. Over the last few decades, I have coached law students and lawyers on how to develop proper trial skills. As a Master Continuing Legal Education Instructor for the New York State Academy of Trial Lawyers, and through my podcast, The Mentor Esq., I have extensively lectured to thousands of attorneys on trial topics including jury selection, opening statements, direct and cross examinations, and closing arguments.

In this book, I discuss the trial from the perspective of a plaintiff in a civil trial, since I have been exclusively a plaintiff's personal injury attorney for more than 25 years. But even if you are a civil defense attorney, or prosecuting or defending in a criminal trial, the fundamental steps for properly preparing and presenting your case at trial remain the same. I have spent my career trying cases in several jurisdictions, but most of my trials have been in the New York State and Federal Courts. Although I cite several New York State specific protocols in this book, the same theories and practice tips will apply regardless of jurisdiction.

This book is designed to break down a trial from start to finish, covering jury selection, opening statements, direct-examination, cross-examination, and closing arguments. I have also included sample materials from my actual trials within, or appended to, each chapter.

With this book, I hope to share and spread the knowledge and experience I have gained throughout my life so that you can improve upon your trial skills and become an even better advocate for your clients.

CHAPTER 1

JURY SELECTION

Every jury trial starts with jury selection, the process of choosing the individuals who will ultimately decide the fate of your client's case. Jury selection is not just about selecting jurors, however. It is equally about removing those individuals who could be a problem if chosen as a juror for your case.

This chapter will discuss:

- Goals for jury selection
- How to prepare
- Creating an outline
- The jury selection process
- The Whites method
- The Struck method
- Notetaking strategies
- Working with your adversary

Goals for Jury Selection

As lawyers, we all want to know how to pick a good jury. There are books, consultants, and continuing legal education (CLE) courses about jury selection. But there's really no strategy or science that can ensure you select a good jury. Ultimately, you have no idea whether you've chosen a good jury. You're thrown into a room of people, trying to find the ones you think will be best for your side of the case, and the chips fall where they may.

I always try to speak with jurors after my trials, and time and time again, I've learned that when I thought I had picked a great jury, I was wrong. The juror who was smiling and nodding at me the whole time, the one I felt was perfect to have in my corner, the one who would bring it home for me, went against me. And on the other hand, some of the people I was most concerned about ended up being in my corner.

The bottom line is, you just don't know. Jurors could be lying when they answer your questions at jury selection. So, you should have three goals for jury selection:

- **Sort out the people you don't want.** That includes people who don't speak English, people who clearly don't want to be there, and people who hate your side of the case. You want to filter out the extreme people and find the ones you think will be most reasonable and sympathetic to your case.

- **Establish credibility with the potential jurors.** The trial doesn't start with meeting the judge or with opening statements. Jury selection is the start of the trial. You are walking into a roomful of people who will decide your case, and they are looking at how you're dressed, how you present, how you're organized, and what you have to say. They are sizing you up, and their opinions will carry all the way through to the verdict.

  So, it's crucial that when you step into that room, you're buttoned up, dressed properly, organized, with your papers in place. You'll want to have your table and notes laid out neatly and have yourself collected and presented. You want to have a nice, clean appearance and make a good impression during jury selection.

- **Address potential weaknesses in your case.** You may have some issues going against you in your case, and you should start to diffuse such issues during jury selection. If there is a glaring weakness in your case that you know your adversary is going to highlight, you can, and should, address it in jury selection.

By way of an example, I once represented a young man who fell onto subway tracks and was run over by the subway train resulting in the loss of his leg. We had a compelling argument that the subway operator could have, and should have, stopped the train before running over my client. We had a major issue, though: blood tests confirmed that our client was completely intoxicated, and that is why he passed out and fell onto the tracks.

7

We knew the defense would argue it was all my client's fault for being drunk and placing himself in a position of danger. So, instead of trying to downplay, or hide from this problem, during jury selection I addressed it head-on. I said to the room full of potential jurors: "You will learn that on the night of the accident, my client was at a bar, drinking alcohol with friends while watching the hockey playoffs. At the end of the night, he walked to the subway to take the train home. He was intoxicated, and that is why he fell from the platform onto the train tracks while waiting for the subway train to arrive. We do not dispute that he was intoxicated. We do not dispute that his intoxication is why he fell onto the train tracks. It is our position, however, that the subway operator should have seen our client and stopped the train before running him over. We believe the evidence will show that the train operator was negligent in failing to timely observe our client and stop the train. A subway operator does not get a "free pass" to run someone over based on the reason the person ended up on the tracks. Subway riders fall on the tracks for various reasons (i.e., slip, medical issues, being pushed). So, I need to know if you are open to the idea that the subway operator could have been negligent even though my client was drunk, OR if the fact that my client was drunk means there is no way you could consider the fault of the train operator."

I asked each potential juror if they could still be fair to my client and consider our arguments. Not surprisingly, some jurors said they could never hold the train operator responsible if our client got drunk and put himself in a position of danger. And guess what? I was able to remove those jurors from sitting on the case *for cause* since they stated they could not be fair. And all the jurors who were selected had to look me in the eye and state that they could be fair and would go into the trial open to hearing arguments and evidence from both sides.

You want to feel comfortable that you've done everything you can to downplay the weaknesses and emphasize the strengths of your case. That should be your mindset in jury selection.

How to Prepare

Before you arrive at the courthouse for jury selection, you need to be prepared. You can't wing it. Preparation for the trial starts with preparing for jury selection. So, I always take the following steps to prepare:

First, I try to get a lay of the land. You may not be comfortable with the area where you're picking a jury. Maybe you've never selected a jury in that courthouse, county, or state, or you just don't know what goes on at that particular courthouse during jury selection.

Go to the courthouse several days before you'll be selecting your jury there. See where the jurors gather and what that day's jury pool looks like. Meet the clerk and the lawyers who are regulars in that courthouse and ask questions about how things work. Don't be embarrassed if you don't know what's going on. Even experienced lawyers are always asking questions, because it's different everywhere. Selecting a jury in one county is different than selecting one in another, and jury selection in Federal Court is different from state court.

At the courthouse, you might want to ask questions like:

- How does the jury process work here?
- Do they use the Whites or the Struck method? (See pages 17 through 20 for details about these two methods.)
- Do they limit your time?
- Does the judge oversee jury selection?
- Is jury selection in the courtroom?
- Will you pick a jury first and then meet your trial judge or vice versa?

Is it "pick and pass," which means you pick a jury, and then return a week or so later to start the trial? Or is it "pick and go," where you pick a jury and get started immediately?

You want to get answers to these questions ahead of time, so you feel comfortable and prepared about the process when you show up for jury selection. Preparation reduces anxiety. Even seasoned lawyers get nervous, but newer lawyers who may have never picked a jury are especially likely to be anxious. Knowing what's ahead can help quell your anxiety.

Creating an Outline

After you have the "lay of the land" at the courthouse, you should create an outline of what you want to cover in jury selection. Spend time thinking about the issues that matter the most for your case, and prepare an outline to aid you in addressing those issues during jury selection.

In a recent trial, I represented a man named Oscar. He was originally from Chile, and English is his second language. He was riding a motorcycle, and when he was turning onto the Grand Central Parkway entrance ramp, a car was turning from the other direction, and they collided. He had serious injuries, including a badly broken leg, and he was hospitalized. He had a stroke in the hospital. He had loss of income.

I had concerns about how Oscar would be perceived if he had to testify through a translator. I was worried a juror might think he was an outsider, not a local or a U.S. citizen (he was both). I was concerned about biases against motorcyclists, since some people think that motorcyclists are troublemakers.

So, here are some things I outlined that I wanted to address during jury selection:

- **How the potential jurors feel about motorcycle operators.** This was a car accident involving a motorcycle and an Audi, and my client was on a motorcycle. So, I want to know if they drive a motorcycle or if they have friends or family members who do. I want to feel out if they have any problems with motorcyclists.

- **Oscar is from a foreign country and will testify through a translator.** I want to make sure my client, a motorcycle operator originally from Chile, is on an equal playing field with locals who live in Long Island and drive cars. I want them to keep an open mind about the fact that he's an immigrant and that he has an accent.

- **Their experiences with serious injuries.** You're allowed to talk about your client's injuries in jury selection. As a plaintiff, you want to do that because, if they are serious injuries, it can help to let the jury know right away. So, I want to talk about the fractured leg, the external fixator, the rod, and the three surgeries. I want to ask if they have ever heard of terms like "fasciotomy." I want to know if they have ever had a serious injury or a fractured leg, or if they or their friends or family members have been hospitalized.
Asking these questions lets them know about the seriousness of your client's injuries and can help gain their sympathy. It's also a way to see if they can relate.

Maybe they had a similar injury, so we talk about that. I'll ask if they've been treated by a physical therapist, orthopedist, or neurologist and let them know that we anticipate hearing from these types of experts at the trial.

- **Where they get their news**. A nice trick I picked up from an adversary at a trial many years ago, before our political discourse became so divergent and extreme, is asking potential jurors where they get their news. I find that, for example, if someone gets their news from MSNBC, they may be more liberal and more pro-plaintiff. If they get their news from FOX, they may be more into tort reform and more against people bringing lawsuits. They may also think that personal responsibility takes precedence, and they may be more worried about taxes, wrongly assuming that settlements impact them. Asking about their news sources, what podcasts they listen to, and what websites they visit is an interesting way to get a sense of which way they may lean politically, which may help you understand which way they may lean in your case.

- **How they feel about compensation for my client.** I'll explain that the way our justice system works is through compensation. I want to get an idea of how they feel about the fact that my client, the plaintiff, is ultimately going to ask for money. If we prove our case, we will ask them to compensate my client. So, I talk to them about whether they have any problems with compensating or any limits in their minds. I want to know how they feel about lawsuits like this—it's essential as a plaintiff to bring this out. If people have issues, you want to get them off of a potential jury. Responding to this question, they could say, "Yeah, I don't have a problem with that." But you have to dig further. You can ask, "Is there a number you think would be too outrageous? Would you ever even think of paying $5 million?" You can throw numbers out there and see how they respond. Someone may roll their eyes, thinking, "Yeah, man, $5 million, you'll have to prove a crazy case to me. Your client better be messed up." Or they may think, "Yeah, I've got no problem. I'm open. I want to hear the proof. And we'll decide it." It's less about

11

the answer and more about their body language and the vibe or feeling you get when they respond.

Ultimately, you want to get jurors who you feel can relate not only to your client, but to you. A lot of jury selection is about getting a good vibe. If I can connect with a juror—if a juror gets me and the way I deliver information—that's going to help my case. So, I'm hoping they're going to connect with my client and with me.

Outlines can be created on computers or iPads, but I prefer to use the good old yellow legal pad to sketch out my jury selection outlines. Here is the outline I prepared for jury selection in Oscar's case:

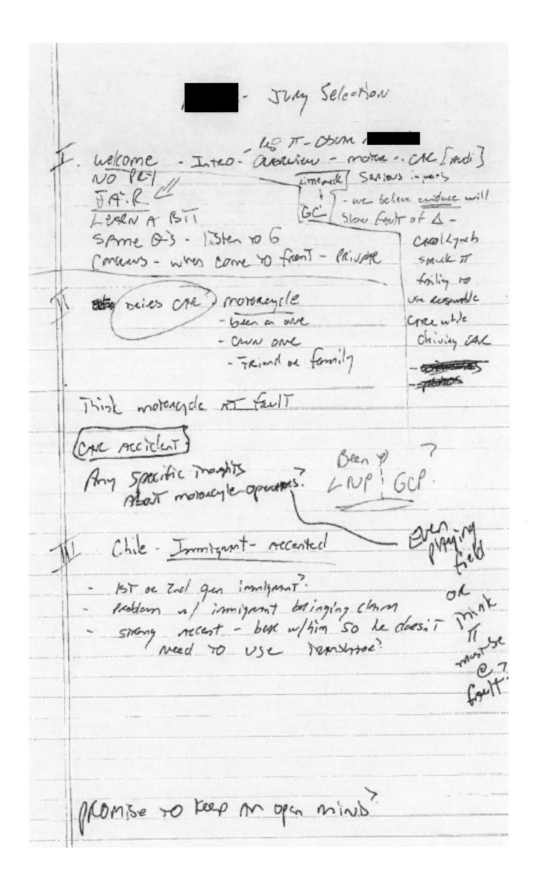

■■■■ - Jury Selection

us π - own ■■■■

I. welcome - Intro - overview - notes . . CAR [and]
NO PI
FAIR
LEARN A BIT
SAME Q's - listen to G
concerns - when come to front - private

Litterick   Serious injuries
           - we believe evidence will
GC   Show fault of Δ -

           Crook/Lynch
           struck π
           failing to
           use reasonable
           care while
           driving car

Π.   ~~does~~ [deies] CAR) motorcycle
              - been a one
              - own one
              - friend or family

Think motorcycle at fault

CAR Accident

Any specific thoughts   Been π   ?
About motorcycle operators? LNP | GCP.

Even playing field

III   Chile - Immigrant - accented

      - 1st or 2nd gen immigrant?
      - problem w/ immigrant bringing claim
      - strong accent - best w/him so he doesn't
              need to use translator?

                                                or
                                                think
                                                Π
                                                must be
                                                @ ?
                                                fault

PROMISE TO keep m open mind?

Jury Selection (2)

II. Injuries   , spinal fracture   lower left leg

- 2nd Phase   ① - fractured rib fib
- medical testimony   ② - rod   ③ stroke
- π testimony   ③ - 3 surgeries
                         ④ - fasciotomy   complication

- Fractured leg? - surgery?] you or
  Hospitalized? [long story] close friend/loved one

  - Impact on your life / friend / family

- Stroke?

- Physical Therapy

- Orthopedist?

- Neurologist?

III. NEWS SOURCE?   ci

Jury Selection (3)

IV. Thoughts on concept of Compensation

- ok w/ position to award money

- prove case   - Can't unring Bell
                      - Civil justice system

If prove serious injuries from accident
    Any problem compensating him?

    Thoughts. - Limit NO matter what
                      - Restitution

Now feel about fact π bringing
    lawsuit? Going to ask to
              be compensated.

The Jury Selection Process

Now that you're prepared and you've outlined what you want to ask, here's the process that *generally* occurs when you arrive at the courthouse for jury selection (keeping in mind that every courthouse operates jury selection a bit differently):

Before you start, the jurors will be pre-screened by the jury part clerk/commissioner, and anyone who shouldn't be on a jury for various reasons will be dismissed. Those who remain will watch some videos about the process.

You'll check in with the clerk and fill out some paperwork that clarifies what the case is about and how many days the trial is expected to last. Then you'll be assigned to a jury selection room. Over the PA system, the clerk will ask approximately 30 or so jurors to report to that room. Each of them will have a big index card with their name and some other information on it.

The clerk will ask the jurors to fill out questionnaires that create multiple copies of their answers so the plaintiff and defense attorneys can review them at the same time. The jurors might fill them out ahead of time, or they may do it once they enter the room. The questionnaires include information like their name, age, address, marital status, employment status, whether they have children, what their children do, hobbies/interests, whether they've ever sued or been sued, and whether they've ever been convicted of a crime.

Once the questionnaires are complete, they're handed to you. With the Whites method, you might get the first six or eight jurors' questionnaires, and with the Struck method, you may get them all. (See below for an explanation of these two methods.) So, you're in a room with about 30 people looking at you, a bin with cards with their names on them, and the questionnaires. And you'll be told to get started. It can be really overwhelming.

The plaintiff and defense counsel (and other lawyers, if there are multiple parties) will be there. If you're the lead plaintiff, you'll address the room of jurors first. It is your opportunity to welcome everyone to jury selection, put them at ease, and explain the process. You want to start by saying something like, "We just received your questionnaires, and we ask for your patience. We're going to take about 10 minutes to go through them, and then we'll begin. So please give us a moment, and we'll be with you shortly."

16

Then you sit down and start going through the questionnaires. The jurors will be seated in a particular order. With The Whites method, they'll be seated in the first six or eight seats in the front. If it's the Struck method, they'll be numbered from 1 through 30 (more or less depending on venue) based on where they're sitting.

The Whites Method

In Oscar's case, I started by addressing the entire jury pool. I said, "Listen, this case has been going on for many years. We can't resolve it and we need your help. I need to go back to my client and let him know that I picked a fair jury. So, if I ask you anything and you feel that I'm prying, I can speak with you outside of the room. But please know that's why I'm asking questions—just to make sure that we have a fair jury for this trial."

I let them know that they're going to learn a little bit about the case. You can give them a brief overview without going into too much detail. Since we were using The Whites method for this trial, I told them that I would speak with the whole panel of jurors first, then bring some up to the front.

Ultimately, there are two ways to pick a jury: The *Whites* method or the *Struck* method. The judge or a judicial hearing officer (JHO), who is often an older, retired judge, chooses the method. It may be different if you're not in New York State, so look for your local court rules. The judge or jury clerk may also have discretion on which method to use. Judges and JHOs can also give you more or fewer challenges—a lot of discretion is permitted.

With the Whites method, you will only ask specific questions of six to eight people at a time. To choose those people, all the cards with the jurors' names are placed in a bin with a wheel that shuffles them, like in bingo. You and/or your adversary will pull six to eight names at random and put those cards into a board called the paddle board or the jury board.

To bring those jurors forward, one lawyer can call all their names, or you can alternate calling them. Have them sit in the front of the room, and ask for their questionnaires.

You'll want to make quick notes based on the questionnaires and their seat number. In The Whites method, you give introductory remarks to the entire room, then you focus on those six to

17

eight jurors. I always tell everybody in the room, "Please listen to the questions we're asking, even though we're not asking them of you specifically. You'll probably be up here in the front row at some point, and you'll be asked the same questions, so you might want to think about what your response will be. Please don't tune out and look at your phone. If you pay attention, it'll save time."

In The Whites method, first the plaintiff will question those six to eight people, one at a time. Then the defendant will question those people. If there are multiple plaintiffs and multiple defendants, they go in order. Everyone gets the opportunity to ask questions.

Sometimes you'll be given time restrictions. The judge, JHO, or jury clerk might tell you that the plaintiff and the defendant each get an hour. If you have multiple plaintiffs or defendants, you'll have to share the time. It's up to you and the other lawyers to agree on how to run things. You all run the show unless you have a problem and need to go to the judge or JHO.

The first round of questions will take longer, and after that, the process gets faster. You'll ask your questions, your adversary will ask questions, then you can ask follow-ups, and your adversary can ask follow-ups. Once that's finished, you can tell the jurors to take a 10- to 15-minute break and remind them to return on time. Then you take the jury board/paddle, step out with your adversary, and find a quiet spot for your first round of challenges.

You have unlimited *cause* challenges. You can use cause challenges when someone clearly is not appropriate to be a juror on the case. An example of a cause challenge might be a person who doesn't speak the language, or makes it clear that they can't be fair. When they answered their questions, they might have said something like, "I was a plaintiff in a personal injury case where I was badly injured. I'd like to be fair, but I really think I'd lean to the plaintiff." Or you may have someone on the defense side who says, "I'd like to be fair, but I think there are too many lawsuits, and there's no way I'm going to want to help this person out. I just don't think I'll be fair." If they say they can't be fair, you can dismiss them for cause.

So, if you want to get someone off for cause, you need them to answer "no" to the question about whether they can be fair. You and your adversary can agree on those removed for cause. If a juror is over-the-top in your favor, you might have to let them go for cause, even if you hate to do it. Because you're going to go back and forth, and there will be someone over the top against

18

you. On your chart, you cross out the people removed for cause, and on the board, you flip over their cards.

Then you get to your *peremptory* challenges, where you can strike anybody for any reason. (There might be *Batson*[1] challenges, where your adversary thinks you don't have a legitimate basis for striking someone other than their race or some other reason, but I've never seen that used in my career.) Generally, the plaintiff and the defendant each have three peremptory challenges. If there are multiple plaintiffs or multiple defendants, they share all three.

The plaintiff goes first and can say, for example, "I want to strike the third person of the six." Then you give the panel to the defense counsel, who can say, "I want to strike this person. He's my peremptory."

If you don't use a peremptory on that first round, you cannot use any more peremptory challenges on that round. Once you say, "I have no peremptory challenges," that means you're good with everybody left on the board after those removed for cause. The same is true for your adversary.

You'll go back and forth. In the first round, you can use none, one, two, or all three of your peremptory challenges. Once you're both done, anybody left who hasn't been struck for cause or a challenge will be a juror. For example, you tell the jury clerk, "We've got two out of the first eight; the rest are for cause or peremptory." The clerk will come into the room, tell those two they will be sworn in as jurors, and the other six will be dismissed from jury duty.

Then, you refill those six to eight seats with new jurors and repeat the process, asking questions again. This time, the defense goes first. After questioning is completed, they'll say who they want to challenge for cause or peremptory. As you go along, there's trading you could do. For example, you might not want to come back another day just to get one remaining juror seat

---

[1] *Batson v. Kentucky* 476 U.S. 79 (1986). In a 7–2 decision, the United States Supreme Court held that, while a defendant is not entitled to have a jury completely or partially composed of people of his own race, the state is not permitted to use its peremptory challenges to automatically exclude potential members of the jury because of their race.

filled. Maybe you can come up with an agreement with your adversary on a juror you can agree upon. These are good conversations to have. You both want a jury that's going to be fair.

You repeat the process until you get six jurors and, usually, two alternates[2]. The alternates could be "designated" or "non-designated." Designated means that the order they're selected as alternates is the order they'll be pulled into the trial if needed. So alternate 1 would be the first alternate used in the trial. Non-designated alternates are selected for the trial at random if needed. So, you won't necessarily know who you're going to get.

The Struck Method

The Struck method is a bit different. With it, all of the potential jurors come into the room. If there are 30 people, there might be three rows of 10, with seats 1 through 10 in the first row, 11 through 20 in the second row, and 21 through 30 in the third row. You'll get all their questionnaires, and you'll need a little more time to review them than with the Whites method, so you might want to give everyone a 20-minute break.

You go through all of your questionnaires and quickly make notes on everyone from 1 to 30. Then the jurors return, and you question the whole room, not just the front six or eight people. The plaintiff goes first, then the defendant, and you both get a turn to ask follow-up questions.

After you've questioned the entire room of potential jurors, you go out with the board and remove all your challenges for cause, then go back and forth through your peremptory challenges. When you and your adversary have both used up your peremptory challenges, or you don't want to use any more, the jurors and alternates are selected based on numerical order. So, jurors number 3, 6, 8, 11, 15, and 18 might be your jury, and 21 and 25 might be your alternates.

Personally, I like the Struck method because I think it's more efficient—you only step out of the jury room once to go through your cause and peremptory challenges. Plus, a little strategy comes into play because you can foresee who your potential jurors might be. In the Whites method,

---

[2] In New York State courts, it is typical to have six jurors and two alternates in civil cases. Sometimes more alternates are selected if it is expected to be a long trial. In criminal trials and in Federal Court the amount of jurors will be different.

you don't know who will fill the seat up front after your first round of challenges. You spin the wheel and call them up. With the Struck method, if you strike someone as a peremptory, you know who's in the following seat. The Whites method tends to be used more often than the Struck.

Notetaking Strategies

You'll want to take notes during jury selection to help you make decisions on who to keep or challenge. The notes are also helpful for you to share information about the jurors you have selected with your client after jury selection is completed. Your client is anxious, and you want to let them know who will be deciding their case. Your notetaking process can help you tell your client whether you think you've selected people who will be fair for their trial or if you feel you have a problem. There may be settlement offers on the table. Maybe a jury doesn't look good for your client. Maybe it looks good. Jury composition may impact settlement discussions. It's important to communicate that with your client.

I learned my method for taking notes the same way I learned pretty much everything else I learned as a trial lawyer, from my father and partner, Guy Smiley. It proved well for him and it continues to serve me well. I know they have apps and preformatted ways to keep everything organized, but I consider myself old-school, and I use legal pads. My notes are kind of haphazard, but there's a method to my madness. I sit down and quickly make a chart. And then, as I get underway, I'll add red notes, circles, and lines. It's a process. You can use your own shorthand, but you want to do it quickly because you have a roomful of people staring at you and waiting for you to get going. And as the plaintiff, you have to do it first. The defense has more time.

In Oscar's trial, the jurors were called into the courtroom and seated in the viewing area. That's where I welcomed everyone and gave my initial interviews. In this case, we used the Whites method, but we filled up the jury box, so instead of six or eight jurors, we brought in 12 at a time to question. In my chart, I started on the bottom left with number 1. My numbers go across to the right up to 6, then up to the left for numbers 7 to 12. I quickly wrote their names in spots 1 to 6 and 7 to 12, and I tried to write notes from their questionnaires, all in black ink. You have to do this fast—it's not easy. It's stressful.

21

The notes I put in black identify their age, gender, background, race, and employment. I want to get as much information as possible about these people because I want to share this information with my client. I want to match people up if there's an opportunity. For example, if my client is African American, my client and I might feel more comfortable with other African Americans on the jury. The same holds true if my client is Asian American, White, or Hispanic.

On the following page, you can see my note chart for the first round of seated people during jury selection using the Whites method. The trial judge had us seat and question 12 people to start (using his discretion to increase the number from six or eight):

- For seat number 1, I wrote the name Chifon, who was a driver for Enterprise. I put down age 50, AA for African American, and a female symbol.
- For seat number 2 I put Salina, female, age 33, who is into marketing.
- Seat number 3, Barbara B., is a 72-year-old retired teacher who lives alone and has testified previously.
- Seat number 4 is a 37-year-old female. Her husband drives a shuttle. They have five girls, and they have been sued before.
- In seat number 5 is Laura, a 38-year-old from Brazil who has been a victim and is worried because she has a doctor's appointment.
- In seat number 6 is a man who's 29, a lawyer and general counsel for a company, and has been sued before.

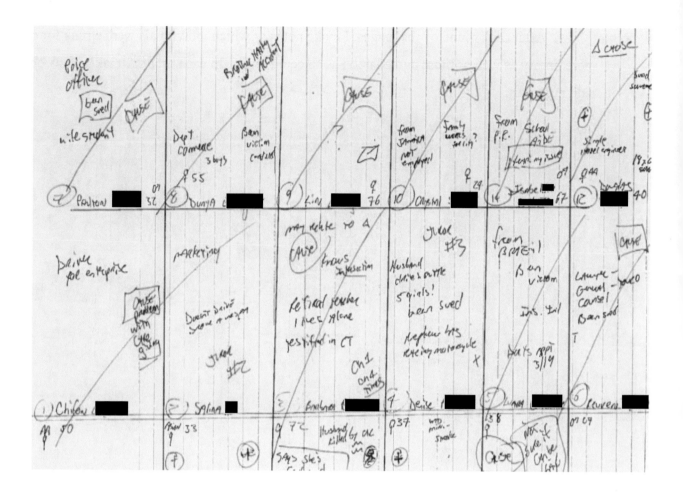

As I go through my outline and question people, I make my notes in red. I'll make all kinds of notes. For example, Salina, number 2, doesn't drive a car. She's driven a Vespa. Do I want someone who's never driven a car in this case? I don't know—maybe she can relate to my client a little more. I write a plus sign. I think she's probably good.

For number 3, Barbara B., I wrote down that she may relate to the defendant. And I wrote "cause" because there's a reason—she says she's confused.

As you look through my notes, you'll see I write "cause" if there's a reason, and I put a plus sign if I like someone and a minus sign if I don't like them for the case. At the end, the lines through names mean my adversary and I agreed to strike those people for cause.

23

After each round of challenges, I make notes of which individuals were struck for cause or peremptory as well as those agreed upon as selected jurors. In each round, I make a new chart and add my notes:

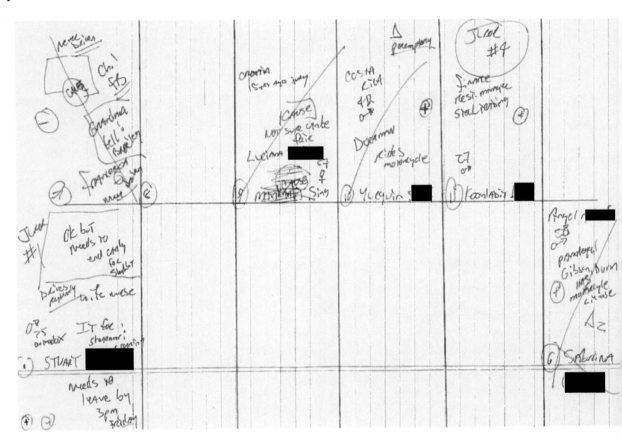

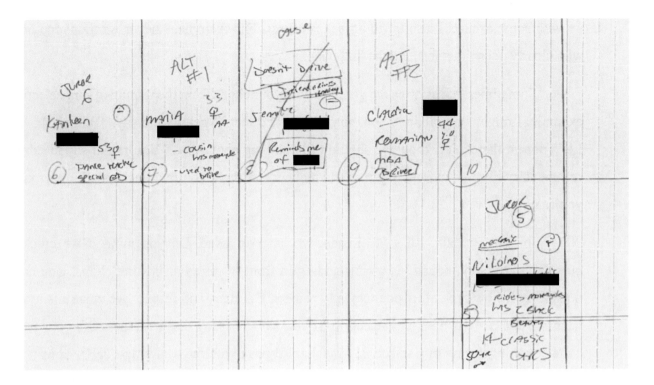

I remember juror number 5 from this case. He was a 50-year-old Greek man who was a mechanic and was really into classic cars and owns motorcycles. I thought he would connect with me and be a good juror. He didn't get struck by the defense, so maybe my adversary thought he would be good for them as well.

Working with Your Adversary

The old-school way to relate to your adversary, which I learned from my father, was to fight like hell in the courtroom, but be friendly and courteous outside the courtroom. You should respect your adversary. They're preparing just like you are, working late at night, and dealing with the same anxieties. Their clients are concerned, and they have to report to them, just like you do. So, you're in the trenches together, and you can respect each other's work and be kind to each other. There's no reason not to. And that starts with the jury selection.

In jury selection, I always talk with my adversary. I try to get an agreement with my adversary to not put anyone on the jury who doesn't want to be there, since it doesn't do any of us any good. We don't want jurors who don't want to be there, who have checked out or are coming up with some excuse. I also try to agree on causes. For example, I never want anyone on a jury who clearly doesn't understand the language.

Sometimes, adversaries are going to bust your chops from the minute of jury selection. For example, I might start talking about something, and they'll get up and say, "Whoa, Mr. Smiley! Let's not go there. You know we shouldn't be talking about that." You're not supposed to have commentary like that in front of jurors and make jurors think you're doing something wrong when you're not.

In that situation, I'll say, "Listen, we have an issue. Do you mind if we quickly step outside?" That way, nobody is grandstanding in front of jurors or busting chops. You can meet outside and show each other courtesy and respect. Courtesy and respect are what this profession is about, and it starts with jury selection. If you have a strong disagreement with your adversary about anything during jury selection, you should speak with the trial judge, JHO, or jury clerk to help resolve the issue. Once the jury has been selected and sworn in, it's time to get ready to deliver your opening statement!

CHAPTER 2

OPENING STATEMENTS

I love opening statements. They are your first chance to make an impression on the jury, your client, the judge, and your adversary. The opening statement sets the tone for the trial ahead. Whether it's going to be a one-day trial or a six-week trial, first impressions count. You want to get off to a good start, for your client and for yourself.

With your opening statement, you can set the stage for a great trial. There's no place where preparation is more critical. Jury selection is the first time that potential jurors see you and get a sense of you. They've heard a little bit about the plaintiff's case and the defense case. Now, in the openings, they're curious. And they're fresh—they haven't been showing up to the same trial for days on end, listening to you and the judge and the witnesses. They're probably at their most alert, and you want to take advantage of that.

Opening statements also give you the chance to get the jury to start viewing the case the way you want them to see it. I like to say, if you want them to see pink, you've got to give them a pink lens to look through. It is essential to point the jury in the right direction during your opening statement.

Think about the opening statement from the jurors' perspective for a moment. They've heard the lawyers posturing in jury selection, they've shown up, and they've been sworn in. They're sitting in the jury box, serious about their jobs as jurors. I compare it to a new movie. You read some previews, go to the theater, get your popcorn, and you're ready for the curtain to open and the show to begin.

That's what the jurors are doing. They're thinking, "Let's see what we've got here. Let's see what this case is going to look like. Let's see what these lawyers are going to do." They're ready for you. So, bring it! You don't want to be a dud. It's your time to shine. If you do it right, you're going to feel good, you're going to get things going, and the case is going to go in a better direction for you.

How to Get More Comfortable with Public Speaking

Let's talk a little bit about public speaking—the presentation part. Many people, and attorneys are no exception, get a little nervous about public speaking, whether they are getting up in front of 10 people or 1,000 people. You're worried that you will mess up, look silly, or ruin the case. But anyone can be great at public speaking, even if you're uncomfortable with it, with a few pointers and some practice.

In your opening statement, you must project a level of confidence. You must interact and be present without looking down and reading your notes. You are not going to look at any notes in your opening statement. You are connecting and speaking to a jury, and you don't want to drop your head down, look away, or read an opening statement. You want to engage. The primary way that you do that successfully is through *preparation*.

But it's also crucial to think about what makes you nervous, and why you are scared or anxious when the judge says, "Counsel, please proceed." It's different for everyone. I get nervous like everybody else does. My nervousness comes from a fear of forgetting what I'm going to say and drawing a blank while all the jurors are waiting and looking at me. I actually have nightmares from time to time, where I'm at trial and I am about to open, but I don't know the facts of the case; I'm looking in my trial file for details about the claim or the injuries; and I wake up in a sweat.

The way I overcome my fears, and the way I suggest you can also overcome your fears, is through preparation. I prepare by having an outline in advance, rehearsing, practicing, and talking out loud, whether I'm speaking to family members, rehearsing in the shower, or talking to one of my many cats. I do what it takes to get myself ready. And I'm not worried about drawing a blank, because I've got my outline off to the side, either at my counsel table, the podium, or on a ledge by the jury box. I've got a safety net while I'm up on the high wire, so I'm not worried.

If you stumble, draw a blank, or are nervous, you can use my "water break" trick. When you're in the middle of an opening (or summation or even in a cross- or direct-exam), and you forget where you're going, or you're not sure what you're going to say next, you just pause confidently, step over to counsel table, grab your water bottle, and take a sip. All the while, you're thinking about what you're going to say. During the brief water break, you can glance at your outline to get back on track. It works for me all the time. When I have my outline ready, and I know I can take my water break, I'm not nervous. If things aren't going as planned, that's my safety net.

And keep in mind, you don't have to have things memorized—you just need to know what you want to say. Practicing speaking helps. Talk to your family or friends about your case. Let them know you're preparing for trial, run stuff by them, and see what they say. It really helps.

You also need to be yourself. When you're preparing for an opening don't think, "I want to present the way Andrew Smiley has presented." I present it the way I present it, and you have to present it the way *you* do. If you come across differently, seem nervous, quiet, or not as interactive, that's OK. It is important to be yourself and not try to act like someone else.

You want the jury to get a sense that you're being honest with them throughout the trial, and that starts during the opening statement. You want to establish credibility, and the best way to do that is to be genuine and be yourself. They'll begin to get to know you through the trial. They'll hear what you have to say in your opening statement. They'll see how you conduct yourself and question witnesses. When you gain credibility from the jury, they will believe in you and your case.

Preparation Strategies

In most of my big cases, I start thinking about my opening statement during the early phases of the litigation. I'm thinking about my opening when I'm questioning witnesses during discovery. I recently handled a medical malpractice–wrongful death case where I deposed numerous doctors. With every critical piece of information I obtained from the witness, I thought about how I would lay it all out in my opening. I could see a theme developing in how they handled my questions, and I was thinking about how to address those issues at trial.

Give yourself sufficient time to prepare an opening statement. You don't want to prepare that morning or the night before trial. Find someplace quiet. If you're in your office and the phones are ringing, or if you're at home with your kids, find a space in your home, a library, a coffee shop, or wherever you can go to tune everyone out. Avoid distractions, turn off your phone, and sit down in a quiet place with your notes and your trial file.

Do some homework to prepare for your opening. Look over the notes you've already made, the photographs, the deposition transcripts, and your other materials, and start noting what you feel is important for your case. Take some time to think about the elements of your case. Look at the Pattern Jury Instructions or specific jury charges in your jurisdiction to see what words the judge will use to charge the jury with the applicable law. You can start incorporating those words right off the bat in your opening statement.

When preparing for your opening statement, you should have your case file with all the transcripts and any notes you've made. Be sure to first review all the evidence, reports, documents, and photos. At this point, I like to go freestyle and write things out as if I'm writing my opening statement. What would I want to say? And how would I say it? I just start writing with a black pen on a yellow legal pad, because I like to write by hand. Then I use a red pen, add boxes, squares, and arrows, and cross things out. It's a process where I just write it all out in a stream of consciousness and make edits as I go back through the outline. This process works so well that by the time I am done I have truly absorbed the content and can even picture the pages of the outline in my head when I'm delivering my opening.

An Example of an Outline

Here is what the outline from my opening statement in Oscar's trial looked like (this was a liability trial only, so there's no section on damages):

OPEN

May it Please the Court ... I am
        I represent π, OSCAR A.

This is a case where the Δ, Carol L█████
failed to use reasonable care and failed
to pay attention while driving her car
on a September Saturday in 2017

- As a result of her failure to use reasonable
care and pay attention that day, she
struck ~~the plaintiff~~ OSCAR while
he was riding on his motorcycle motorcycle,
propelling - knocking him to the ground and causing landed on off
him him to be seriously injured and his leg
into a skidded ~~ACCENT~~
forward skid while his trapped
leg beneath motorcycle

The 1st witness you will here from is OSCAR A.
Birthday Yesterday! - You will learn that OSCAR is a 6̶0̶ 70 man
who is originally from Chile - South America
he moved to the U.S. many years ago and
U.S. Citizen for the last 20 years he has lived and
worked here in Queens as a handyman
for a large apt. complex. Hyde Park
Gardens

COOL Harley DNA Super- Glide - 19 years ago he purchased *prized possession* his Harley Davidson
motorcycle. A motorcycle he has taken
great pride in. Only takes out on
special occasions when the weather
is good.

- Takes motorcycle to charity events and
fundraisers to help raise money for
cancer and children.

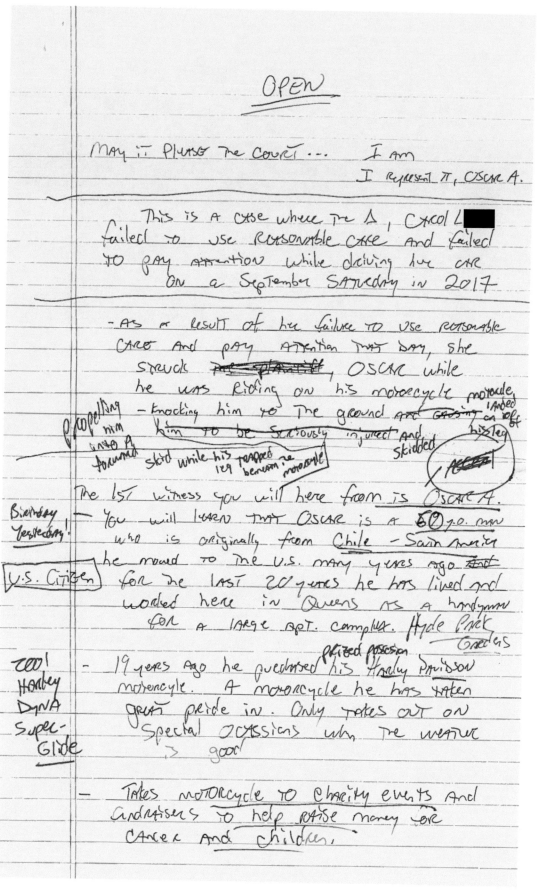

31

Open
(c)

(D/A)
Learn that on "~~Saturday~~ Beautiful day, September 23,
2017

Oscar was on his way to one
of these benefits — to raise money
to help Autistic children

[Harley pointed back
and parked in Queens]

to get to benefit he had to ~~get~~ ride
from his home on 138th St in
Queens to the GCP westbound

The Route brought him to the intersection
of LNP & the GCP Service Road

Learned that while travelling on LNP
As he approached int, he brought his
Harley to a brief stop then, when not
seeing any oncoming traffic towards
him, he turned left on GCP
Service Road
- He wasn't speeding — taking it easy
going about 20mph
looking ahead while going
straight on GCP service Rd towards
entrance to GCP

- felt a hit on the back right side
of his Harley then another hit
which knocked him and his Harley
over where he crashed to the ground
under his Harley and skidded until
he came to a stop with entire
left of Harley on top of his leg
when hit and knocked him to
- looked back from position on ground
and saw a (Black Audi)

32

OPEN
(3)

The Defendant

The Black Audi, you will learn
was ~~being~~ being driven by

owned by a man name Phillip █████
        but on this day it was being
driven by his wife, Carol █████

Evidence will show that Δ, Carol █████
was 100% responsible for this accident
b/c she failed to pay attention
                use reasonable care
while driving Audi

Evidence will show that she was
(1) driving too fast
(2) not paying attention and failed
to ~~seeing~~ what was there to
    be seen ~~around her~~ while
while driving
~~███~~

Oscar did nothing wrong

Closing   Open
                            (4)

I am confident that if you pay
close attention to the evidence
presented at this trial

    you will ~~conclude~~ conclude that
    the ∆ was not using
    reasonable care and
    failed to pay attention

    Cause of the accident
        on 9/23/17   thank you.

    we will present evidence for you
    to evaluate in this case about
    the accident and the ∆'s failure
    to use reas. care & failure to
    pay attention.

OSCAR → Photos of [Accident, Scene / Harly & Audi]
CAROL → pay attention to her description of
        events and whether they changed
        since the day of accident
        until today

[∆ Defense NOT CORRECT]

    ~~was~~ I think the evidence
        will show that she has
        changed her story
Carol's husband → here what she told him
Accident Reconstructionist → Diagram and scientifically
    ⚓   explain how accident
    inspected Harley   occurs
    confirmed damage from ∆'s foot bumper

34

You can see in my outline what I have right off the bat: "May it please the court…." "I am… and I represent…." I'm putting down what I'm going to say.

People ask, "Do you really have to do the 'May it please the court?' Why take up the time doing that? Why don't you just get right to it?" The answer is, that's my style. I feel it gives me structure and stability. You don't have to do it that way. If you think it's better to get right to it, get right to it.

Next is my theme. I didn't have a great theme. So, I wrote, "This is a case where you'll learn that the defendant, Carol L., failed to use reasonable care and failed to pay attention while driving in her car on a September Saturday in 2017." And there's a reason I chose the words "reasonable care" because that's in the jury charge. So, I want them to start hearing "failure to use reasonable care."

Then I go to my next block. "As a result of her failure to use reasonable care and pay attention, she struck…." And, I have "the plaintiff," and I crossed it out. I wanted to say "Oscar" to personalize it. I wrote, "She struck Oscar while he was riding on his motorcycle, knocking him to the ground." I originally put, "and causing him to be seriously injured." But that sounded kind of bland. So, in the red note, I changed it to "propelling him into a forward skid while his leg was trapped beneath the motorcycle. And the motorcycle landed on top of him and skidded." This is my process. I'm crossing things out, looking at them, and thinking of stronger ways to say things.

Then I got into what the jury was going to hear, and I personalized it. He's a 60-year-old man. He's originally from Chile. It was his birthday yesterday. I made a point of saying he's a US citizen, in case any jurors think he's an illegal immigrant who's milking the system. For the last 20 years, he's worked in Queens as a handyman in an apartment complex. You start personalizing it. I know a lot of people in New York City live in buildings with superintendents, and everybody likes their supers because they take care of them.

I talked about how, 19 years ago, he got his prized possession, a Harley Davidson Dyna Super Glide. Motorcycle riders probably know what that is. But I'm bringing up the point that this is his prized possession. He doesn't go out there like a young punk, ride, and cut people off. He only takes it to charity events. At his deposition, he testified that he was on his way to one of these charity events to raise money for autism with his fellow Harley riders.

I talked about this beautiful day, when he was going to Alley Pond Park in Queens to raise money for autistic children, bringing his prized possession. I spoke about the route to get onto the Grand Central Parkway, leading him right up to the accident.

Then I get into the evidence: "You will learn that while he was traveling on Little Neck Parkway, he briefly stopped, then turned left on the service road to get onto the Grand Central Parkway. He will tell you. You'll hear from Oscar. He wasn't speeding. He was going about 20 miles an hour. He was looking ahead, taking it easy, when out of nowhere, he felt a hit in the back, he felt it twice, and it knocked him down."

"Next thing he knew, he was on the ground, struck from behind, sliding with this huge motorcycle on top of him, until it finally came to a stop. He looked back to see what happened. And he saw the defendant. He saw a black Audi sedan. You will learn that the defendant, Carol L., was driving this black Audi sedan at the time, which was owned by her husband, Philip L.."

This is the preview. I said things like, "Here's what you're going to learn. She was 100% responsible." I wrote in 100% because this was a case where we agreed to a cap to a top number. If the jury found it was all Oscar's fault, he would get nothing. If they found it was 100% the defendant's fault, we'd get the whole amount. And if it was 50-50, we'd get whatever percentage we could prove.

So right in my opening, I was saying she was 100% at fault. She failed to use reasonable care. The evidence would show that she was driving too fast and failed to pay attention. She failed to see what was there to be seen. I used that phrase because it's another charge a jury will get. And I said, "Oscar did nothing wrong. He did absolutely nothing wrong."

I added in additional notes before I finished. And I said, "I'm confident you will conclude that she was 100% at fault. She failed to use reasonable care, and she was the sole cause of this accident."

I talked about how the evidence will show that she changed her story: "Keep an eye out for that. Listen to what her husband says she told him from the scene. Listen to what she says she told

36

him from the scene. You're going to hear from an accident reconstructionist who's scientifically going to explain to you what happened. Thank you." And then I ended.

The outline on the preceding pages may look completely disorganized to you, but it worked great for me! That is the key. Make an outline that helps *you* know what you want to say. You are creating the outline for yourself and nobody else. You can do it on a laptop or computer—you need to do what works for you. It doesn't have to be my way if that's not how your mind processes things. But whatever you do, just do a free-flow session. Sit down and start writing or typing your thoughts out.

Look for a Theme

As you're writing or typing, start thinking about a theme. It's good if you can find a theme that can be used throughout the case. In the last chapter, I mentioned a subway accident case where my client, Dustin, fell onto the subway tracks and was run over by a train and lost his leg. He was intoxicated at the time. It was a tough case. And I came up with a theme: "If you see something, do something."

I came up with that theme because I was taking the subway to work every day, and I saw these signs in the New York City transit system that said, "If you see something, say something." It was a message that encouraged people to say something to transit workers or the police if they saw bags left unattended or suspicious things happening. So, my theme for that case was, "If you see something, do something" because, in his deposition, I got the train operator to admit that he saw something on the tracks and thought it was garbage when in fact, it was my client. He had a chance to do something—to put on the brakes, to slow down—and he didn't until it was too late. I brought that theme out right at the start of my opening statement. And I included it throughout my questioning and in summation. A full transcript of my opening statement from Dustin's case can be found in the Appendix to this chapter.

If you can find a theme, be creative. Workshop it with family members, colleagues, and friends. You can bring it right out and start the opening statement with it. It could be simple. If it's an auto accident case, you can say, "This is a case about driver inattention."

37

Not all cases lend themselves to themes, but if you can come up with one, it's a great method. It'll help you. It'll help the jury follow along. You can carry it through questions and cross-examination. In my train case, when I was questioning their subway expert, I said, "You'd agree, right? If the operator sees something, they must do something, right?" There are ways to carry your theme throughout.

I have an eight-point outline that I recommend for sketching out an opening statement:

Outline Part 1. *"May It Please the Court"*

Your outline should always start the same way. If you look back at every trial I've had, all of my opening statements start the exact same way. When the judge indicates they're ready for the plaintiff to present an opening statement, I stand up. I make sure I'm buttoned up. I look at the judge, and I use my same format, saying, "May it please the court." You've all heard that phrase. With it, you're saying, "Welcome to the show, folks."

Then I address the court: "Thank you, Your Honor. Judge Stallman, Counsel." I turn to my adversary and members of the jury, and I look at the jury. I say, "Good morning. My name is Andrew Smiley, and I represent the plaintiff, Dustin." Even though they likely know your name from jury selection, you can still say it again. And then, I put my hand out toward my client, and I have my client prepared to nod, sit up a little bit, or look and smile at the jury.

By doing that same intro for every single opening statement, I know I will get off to a good start. I know what I'm going to say, and I'm unlikely to fumble it. I know it'll get me started, and I'll be off and running. With it, you're not worried about what to say or how to start your opening. It's a good, appropriate, professional way to start.

Outline Part 2: *Your Theme*

Next, if you have a theme, go right to it. In the example I gave, I turned to the jury and said, "If you see something, do something." They looked at me like they were thinking, "What the hell is he saying?" And then I say it again, "If you see something, do something. That's what this case is about, members of the jury. If you see something, do something. You will learn that…" and then I got into it, giving an overview of the case: "You'll learn that my client on this date was

38

struck by a subway train, and the operator saw something on the tracks, but failed to do anything. He *saw* something. But he didn't *do* something, and he should have."

Outline Part 3: "You Will Learn That…"

People always ask me whether you can say, "You will learn that…" since you're not supposed to say things that could be considered evidence and draw an objection. In your opening statement, you should be safe, as long as you preface it with, "You will learn that…" or "We expect the evidence to show that…" or "We intend to prove that…." You just need that little preamble. Instead of saying, "The driver was totally at fault for blowing the stop sign," you should say, "We intend to establish that the driver was totally at fault for blowing the stop sign." And if you get an objection in your opening statement, keep your cool. Look back at the jury and say, "We believe the evidence will prove that…" and keep going.

You'll get into your client's background. So, in my example, I said, "You will learn that my client, Dustin, is 25 years old. And on the night of this accident…." Then you talk about your client. This is the time when you humanize your client, which is critical to do throughout a trial.

Outline Part 4: The Events

Next, you talk about the events leading up to the accident. So, after I spoke a little bit about Dustin and who he was, I said, "And you will learn that on the night of April 22nd, he was out with friends watching a hockey game. And yes, they were drinking. But he knew it wasn't safe for him to drive home, and he couldn't afford a car service. So, he did what all New Yorkers do—he took the subway. He was standing on the subway platform, and that's the last thing he remembers before waking up in the hospital without part of his leg."

Outline Part 5: The Accident

Here, you describe the details of the accident in a manner most favorable to your client's perspective. For example: "You will learn that a subway train was approaching the station where my client had fallen on the tracks. You will learn that Dustin was not hidden under the platform, but was right between the two rails the train was traveling along where he could be seen by the

39

train operator. You will learn that, as the train was entering the train station, the train operator saw Dustin lying there on the tracks, but thought he was just some garbage or debris, so he didn't slow the train." It is important to be descriptive, as if you are telling a story. You want the jury to start visualizing the accident based on the details and imagery you provide to them.

Outline Part 6: Negligence & Liability

After I explain the details of the accident, I use the following transition statement: "This accident never should have happened, but for the negligence of the defendant." Then you prove why the defendant is liable. In my example, I said, "My client never should have lost his leg. You will learn that the train operator was negligent because he should have slowed the train, even if he thought it was only garbage on the tracks. You will also learn that if he slowed the train as required, he could have stopped the train before running Dustin over. You will learn what happened as a result of this negligence from the defendant. You will learn that the ambulance showed up...." And then you move on to the damages.

Outline Part 7: Damages

It is important to give a thorough overview of the anticipated evidence you expect to introduce regarding the plaintiff's damages. Damages include economic damages, such as loss of income and medical expenses, as well as non-economic damages, such as pain and suffering and loss of enjoyment of life. Let the jury know if your client was hospitalized, had surgery, or has scarring. I always like to give the jury a preview of the serious injuries sustained and the impact those injuries have had on my client's life.

Outline Part 8: Wrap Up

You want to finish your opening statement strong—start strong and finish strong in openings, summations, and whenever you're engaging directly with the jury. Repeat your theme, make eye contact with the jury, and thank them in advance on behalf of yourself and your client for their attention. Then, sit down.

Practice, Practice, Practice

Once you've prepared this outline, it's time to practice. Like 99.9% of what I know, I learned this method from my father, Guy Smiley. These building blocks are proven, tried and true throughout his career and mine.

If I have an intro and a theme that I'm happy with, I'll practice when I'm walking around in my house or outside, driving my car, or taking a shower. I start with, "May it please the court, …" and I go through, "Members of the jury, this is a case about…" and I mention my theme. Once I feel comfortable saying those parts without having to look at my outline, I start talking about my client's background. And then, I've got my intro, my theme, and my client's background, and I feel comfortable talking about it. I know it all.

Then I get to the events leading up to the accident. And I continue talking out loud. I practice it. It doesn't have to be exact. You're not supposed to have something that you read or regurgitate verbatim—that's not the idea. You just want to trigger in your mind the things you already know. You need to talk about it. Writing it out or typing it out causes you to really think about what you want to say. Then you practice it with the building blocks.

Once you do that enough, you'll be ready to rock and roll when it's time to deliver your opening statement. And if you miss something, you forget, bumble, or draw a blank, you've got your outline nearby. You take your sip of water, you look at the outline, and you jump right back in. That's the proper way to prepare for your opening statement.

If you present an opening statement and you're looking down or reading, you'll lose the jury. They're going to tune you out. You need to practice engaging. If you go through the process correctly and you've taken the time to prepare, when you get up there, it's like you're giving an opening statement on steroids.

When I present my opening statement, I visualize my outline—I see that yellow pad with my black markings and my red circles and arrows in my head. I'm speaking it, and I know where I'm going on the outline, because I've written it, marked it, and discussed it in my head and with whomever I practiced it with.

How Long Should Opening Statements Be?

I get a lot of questions about the length of opening statements. There's a school of thought that your opening should be short, and you're not allowed to talk about evidence. You should just get up there, briefly touch on things, and sit down. I strongly disagree with that school of thought. You want to take advantage and use as much time as you need to lay out your case because a jury will hear what you say in opening. Don't rush. Be thorough.

If I say, "I intend to prove to you that he didn't have that much to drink," maybe it doesn't come out through a witness. But when it's time for deliberations, maybe someone on the jury says, "Wait, he didn't have that much to drink." Whatever it may be, you want to lay it out in opening. It's your chance to give the jury a teaser of what you want them to think about. So, take your time.

In a unified trial (not bifurcated) I'll often have 10 or 11 pages outlined on my legal pad, and I'll take a half an hour or forty minutes to deliver an opening. The jury will know everything I want them to know about the case. It previews what they're going to hear from the witnesses. If I deliver it properly and effectively, it's not too long or boring.

When I finish, nine times out of 10, my adversary will get up and say, "Well, Mr. Smiley gave a very eloquent opening statement, members of the jury, but you haven't heard any of the evidence, right? We talked about that in jury selection. We strongly disagree with Mr. Smiley, and we intend to show that. Just because you heard it from Mr. Smiley now doesn't mean it's really evidence, or you're even going to hear it at the time of the case. Thank you so much."

I hear that a lot. And it's a blown opportunity by defense counsel. I've taken advantage of the stage and platform provided for a commanding opening statement. I've made my point. I've laid out the case, while my adversary fails to do so and loses the opportunity. If you're a defense attorney, you need to humanize your client in any way you can. If you have a corporate defendant, you need to show that they're not the big bad defendant, but that there are people behind the company. They're individual defendants, and the jury needs to hear their stories.

In Dustin's case, I had an excellent adversary, and he probably said something like, "You'll learn what it takes to become a subway operator, how hard it is, and the work that goes into it. You'll learn what it's like to be in a tunnel all day long when it's pitch black. And as much as Mr.

Smiley wants you to think that this one moment in time should have been so clear, it's not like that. You'll hear what it's like." The defense needs to bring it equally in opening. Good defense lawyers do that.

Engaging with the Jury Can Make a Difference

Here's an example of engaging with a jury during an opening statement: I had a product liability case in the Southern District of New York. My client was a personal trainer from Germany attending the International Personal Training Conference. He was exercising in the gym of the Hilton Hotel, doing bench presses with dumbbells with his back on an exercise ball. The ball burst, he fell, and the weights went back and broke both of his wrists.

So, in my opening statement, I demonstrated what happened as best as I could. I was arching back, turning sideways, pretending to hold up the weights. I wanted the jurors to picture exactly what was going on when the accident occurred. I gave a really strong opening statement, the case went well, and we ended up settling the case right before summations.

Six months later, I was on vacation. And I happened to run into the president of the company that made this product—basically, the defendant. It was kind of awkward. I said, "Oh, hello, sort of weird to see you here, but nice to see you." She was with her daughter. She turned to me and said, "I've got to tell you something funny. We were sitting in the courtroom, and the trial was starting, and you gave your opening statement. And at the end of your opening statement, my daughter leaned over to me and said, 'Mom, you guys are in big trouble here.'"

It's a fun anecdote. But the point is, if you start off strong, your adversary is going to know they're going to have their hands full. The judge will know you know what you're doing. The jurors are going to say, "This lawyer is good. We're going to pay attention." That's important.

How to Make a Good Impression

Think about how many times you're at a continuing legal education seminar or in a classroom setting, and you get a little bored, so you look around. I know there are times when people are checking out my clothes, my pocket hanky, or my bald head. People look around. They're going to look at your counsel table. And they might think, "Look at that guy. He's got his

43

shirt hanging out of his pants. He didn't even tie his shoes. The papers are all over the place. This guy's a mess."

That carries over. So, make sure you're neat and organized. Take your wallet, phone, and other things out of your pockets and put them away in your bag or briefcase. Turn off your phone and put it in your bag. You don't want to be in the middle of an opening statement with something vibrating, ringing, or dinging. I'm not a fan of having a pen in your hand—it's distracting if you're moving your hands. Don't hold your pad, outline, or anything else in your hand. Keep your outline either on your table, at the podium if there is one, or on the ledge by the jury box. You can get to it if necessary, but it's not a distraction.

Put on your good clothes. Dress nicely but not flamboyantly. For women, I don't like too much jewelry. For men, ensure your shirt is buttoned and tucked in, your tie is up, and you're ready to go. Make sure your counsel table is clean, with your pad and files where they need to be and everything in its place. You are presenting for your client, and the jurors look at that.

Tips for Presenting Strong Opening Statements

You can do a few things during your presentation to make your opening statement as powerful as possible.

- **Eye contact.** When you get up to present, make eye contact with the jurors. To do that without making them feel awkward, leave enough space. Don't get too close to the jury box whenever you're presenting a case, whether it's opening, on cross-examination, or on summation. You don't want to invade someone's personal space by getting too close to them.

Scan the jurors and make sure you look at everyone when you're talking. You may want to pause, make eye contact with one juror for a moment, and give a nod while you're speaking. Then move on to the next. Don't hold eye contact too long with any one person, but make sure they're seeing you and hearing you. That's how you communicate, not by looking down and reading. It's by being engaged. You want the jurors to listen to what you're saying, and that's the best way to do it.

- **Avoid the podium, if possible.** If there's a podium, you might not know what to do. Do you have to use it? Is it just for examining your witnesses? Is it for the opening statement? Don't feel awkward. Ask. I always ask the judge, "Your Honor, I see there's a podium. Does Your Honor have a preference on whether we use it or don't use it during openings and summations or in our examinations?" Some judges will say you can use it if you want; if not, you can move it out of the way. Some will say, "For all witnesses, I want you to be at that podium, but you don't need to use it for openings." Some say, "You don't need it at all," or "You need it always."

If you don't need to be stuck at the podium for an opening statement, leave it to the side. You can put your outline on it and then step away. You want to be in the well—the area in front of the jury box—when you are engaged with the jury. You want them to hear what you have to say.

So, leave your notes off to the side, move the podium out of the way, and get into the well. You can walk a little bit. You can move from side to side. You don't need to be static. You can use your hands. I love to use my hands—it's just how I talk. If you don't, and you want to keep your hands clasped behind you or in front of you, that's fine. Do what feels right for you and what will make you most comfortable when presenting your case.

- **Vary your tone of voice.** You may want to change your inflections so that when it's something really important, you get the jury's attention. For example, in my personal trainer case, I said, "You're going to learn that while he was in the middle of doing a press up, BOOM, this ball burst, he crashed to the ground, his wrists flew back, and he was an extreme pain." And then I brought it down a notch and said, "Can you imagine how that felt?"

"Next he knows, people are running to his aid, and the ambulance is showing up." Practice increasing your volume, decreasing it, or making clapping sounds. These are all techniques to keep a jury engaged.

By the time I was done with my opening statement, I had made the bang, I did the ball bursting, and I was demonstrating things. The jurors already have it in their heads. They've seen it. So, when my client or experts are on the stand explaining it, they've had that preview already. It's very effective.

- **Emphasize your strengths and address your weaknesses.** Every case has strengths and weaknesses on both sides. Opening statements are an excellent opportunity to address your strengths and weaknesses and give the jurors a little preview of something you think is good in your case or something to look out for.

Here's an example. In Oscar's case, I knew from the pre-trial depositions that the driver's husband testified that his wife called him from the scene of the accident and told him that she hit a motorcyclist. In her deposition, the wife denied that she struck the plaintiff and denied telling her husband that she did.

So, in my opening, I said, "When you're sizing up this case, I want you to size up my client. It's your job to size everybody up, to see who's credible, whose versions are credible, and who's aren't. And I want to give you a little heads up. When I ask the driver what she said to her husband when she called him from the accident scene, and when I ask her husband what she said, pay very close attention to their answers. Because I expect that you will be surprised, and you may question the credibility of what they have to say. So just be on the lookout for that." That's fun to do.

If it's a weakness, bring it out, too. Don't wait for your adversary to do it. Suppose you have a construction accident case, and your client is a laborer who was in prison but who was able to get a job in construction, as many ex-cons do.

Maybe the defense talked about it in mediation and said, "We don't think a jury is going to want to give an ex-con…." Bring it out in your opening. Tell the jury, "You're going to learn something in my client's background. You're going to learn that he was in prison." You can say it however you want.

46

And then, if the defense decides to go down that road, you can say, "What does that have to do with anything? He did his time, he got out, and he got a job. He was working hard, but due to a lack of safety protection, he wasn't protected. The fact that he was in prison when he was younger has nothing to do with this case. Don't take your eye off the ball here."

So, bring out any weaknesses and figure out how you will present them. It could be bad, but better to have it come from you. If you have a strength, bring that out, too.

Final Thoughts on Opening Statements

By the time I'm done writing everything out, making my points, practicing it, and thinking about what's important, when I get up, I see my red pen marks. I'm remembering that I added "skidded and slid." I've got it all there, and I'm delivering it. And if I need to regroup, I take a sip of water, look at my outline, and get back to it.

Taking the time to properly prepare and practice delivering your opening statement virtually guarantees a successful start to the trial.

CHAPTER 2 APPENDIX

MY OPENING STATEMENT IN DUSTIN'S CASE

2   MR. SMILEY: Thank you, your Honor. May

3   it please the Court, Judge Stallman, Mr.

4   G, members of the jury, good afternoon.

5   Nice to see you all again.

6   For those of you who ride the subway,

7   there is a phrase the Transit Authority has been

8   using lately, if you see something, say

9   something. Okay. They put it all over the

10   place, in the trains and on the platform. In

11   this case the phrase is if you see something, do

12   something. Unfortunately, for my client, Dustin,

1   the train operator saw something but he

2   didn't do something.

3   Now, as the judge told you, I would like

4   to reintroduce myself, I'm Andrew Smiley. This

5   is Dustin seated right here (indicating).

6   The woman seated next to Dustin is him mom, Susan

7   and her other son, Dustin's brother, Nick.
8
9   You're going to get to meet Dustin,

10   perhaps as earliest as today, and you'll hear a

11   little bit about him. A little bit about the

12   person he is and who he is now.

13   You'll learn that Dustin grew up in a

14   small town outside of Buffalo to a very close

15   family, where he's the youngest of three boys.

16   And he lived at home with his parents and his

17   older brothers outside of Buffalo. Went to high

18   school there. Was educated there. He was an

19   excellent student and athlete growing up and

20   through high school.

21   You'll learn he played all kinds of

22   sports, soccer, football, basketball and he

23   played varsity sports in high school. When he

24   was a senior in his high school year, the high

25   school voted him as the high school senior

26   athlete of the year. And he graduated from high

1   school doing well and went to college, to a small

2   university called Utica College in upstate New

3   York.

4   He continued his studies in his athletics

5   when he went on to college at Utica College and

6   obtained a degree in Bachelor of Science in an

7   area known as economic crime and criminal

8   justice. You'll learn this is an area that

9   Dustin had always wanted to get into to be an

10   investigator, a crime fighter. He had aspired to

11   be a state trooper or perhaps an FBI agent or

12   Secret Service specialist.

13   In college not only did he excel in

14   academics but in athletics. He was a varsity

15   letterman. He played varsity football his

16   freshman year. He played a lot of positions.

17   One position he's very proud of was kicking field

18   goals. Back then he had a very viable and very

19   strong right leg that he used to kick the ball to

20   the upright to much success.

21   After his freshman year he played varsity

22   football -- basketball rather for three years.

23   And he excelled in both of those sports.

24   When he graduated from college, he

25   graduated with honors, something known as cum

1   laude, which is a very high degree of honors of

2   graduation. Then he did, back in 2005, what many

3   young people do when they graduate from college

4   outside of the city, he decided to move to the

5   big city to start his adult life with a degree

6   and pursue his dreams. And that's what he did.

7   You'll learn in 2005, after graduation,

8   Dustin moved to Staten Island, and he applied for

9   internships to pursue his career in

10   investigation, and he got an internship with HIP,

11   the insurance company, in their investigation

12   unit, and look for fraud, insurance fraud and

13   that type of work. Finally he was able to get a

14   paying job. And he secured a job with Bergdorf

15   Goodman, the high end retail store in New York

16   City, where he worked again in their

17   investigation and theft loss department, where he

18   looked for shoplifters. He looked for employees

19   that were trying to steal goods and that type of

20   work. You'll learn, members of the jury, that it

21   was that job he was at immediately prior to the

22   happening of the accident that we're going to be

23   talking about in this case.

24   It was a Saturday, April 22nd of 2006.

25   And Dustin worked that Saturday at Bergdorf

1   Goodman. It's a Saturday. So, it's a retail

2   store. It was open. You'll learn that Dustin

3   was there all day doing his job, and the store

4   closed about 7 o'clock. And after wrapping

5   everything up, it was time to go out. It was

6   Saturday night.

7   You'll learn that back then, he is 25

8   now, he's **22** then, he did what many young, single

9   people do **in** the city on a Saturday, he went out

10   with friends. That's what he did. He caught up

11   with an old friend of **his**, a woman by the name of

12   Nikki D. You'll get to meet Nikki

13   during this trial. And Dustin spoke with Nikki,

14   and they arranged to meet up to go out on the

15   Upper West Side.

16   Dustin and Nikki go way back to their

17   childhood days. They dated on and off and they

18   stayed friends into their adulthood. Nikki was

19   out with some friends and invited Dustin to join

20   them for some drinks at a bar at the Upper West

21   Side.

22   You'll learn Dustin left work, and he

23   went up to go meet Nikki and some other people on

24   the Upper West Side at a bar. When he arrived

25   there, Nikki was there, some of her friends and

1   colleagues were there. They had a table in the

2   back. They had some pitchers of beer and Dustin

3   joined in. He spent some time there, for a

4   couple of hours, drinking beer, hanging out with

5   Nikki and meeting some friends, making some

6   friends, all right.

7   You'll learn he was there for a few

8   hours, again drinking beer, hanging out. And

9   then after a period of time they decided to go

10   someplace else. The crowd shrunk to just Dustin

11   and Nikki and another friend, another gentleman.

12   The three of them went to another place in the

13   same area. They walked over to another bar.

14   There was a hockey game going on at that time

15   playoffs, I believe. And they went to go watch

16   the hockey game and spend some more time on the

17   Saturday night.

18   They continued to drink. He drank some

19   more beers. It became late at night, sometime

20   after 1 o'clock, and they decided to call it a

21   night and everybody head home, all right.

22   At the time Dustin was living in Staten

23   Island. So, you'll learn the way he would get

24   home, being 22 and not having the benefit of car

25   service or to afford a cab to take you from the

1   Upper West Side to Staten Island, was public

2   transportation. So, what he would do is take the

3   N train down to Whitehall or South Ferry, where

4   you get the Staten Island Ferry. And then he

5   would take the Staten Island Ferry to Staten

6   Island to get home.

7   On that night Nikki and her friend had to

8   go to New Jersey. So, their intention was to

9   take the Path Train to get back to New Jersey.

10   You'll learn they left that second bar,

11   and it was pouring rain out. And what they did

12   is they hopped a cab, all of them, to get down

13   town, to get closer to the train, to 14th Street.

14   And, that's what they did. They got a cab. They

15   took it down. You'll learn the reason why nobody

16   took the cab home is frankly, you know, it's hard

17   enough to get a cab driver to take you to Staten

18   Island or New Jersey, and if you're fortunate to

19   get one, it's expensive, it's very expensive to

20   do that. Certainly if you're a 22-year old.

21   They took the cab down and they all got

22   out to go their own ways. You'll learn that

23   Dustin was going into the 14th Street subway

24   station you've heard us talk about to get the N

25   train, all right.

1   You'll hear from Dustin and Nikki that

2   Dustin had a lot to drink that night. We don't

3   dispute that at all okay. Certainly he was in

4   control of himself. He wasn't slurring. He

5   wasn't stumbling. He was managing just fine.

6   Most importantly, members of the jury, he wasn't

7   driving a car, okay.

8   We anticipate you're going to hear a lot

9   of talk about intoxication levels, numbers and

10   values. This is not a case where he did anything

11   illegal, all right. He didn't get behind the

12   wheel of a car. He didn't attempt to drive. He

13   took public transportation. And you'll hear from

14   Dustin and from Nikki that he was certainly in

15   good enough shape to do that, to walk down, get

16   on a train and take the train to a boat to get

17   home.

18   You'll learn, members of the jury, that

19   that is the last thing that Dustin remembers from

20   that evening. He does not remember the happening

21   of the accident at all. No memory from the time

22   that he got out of that cab in the rain to go to

23   the train. The next thing he remembers after

24   saying goodbye to Nikki that night is waking up

25   in the emergency room in Bellevue, when they were

1   popping his left hip back into his socket, the

2   leg that did not get amputated.

3   There is no one that will tell you what

4   happened in this case, of how Dustin ended up on

5   the tracks. We don't know. There are no

6   witnesses that saw it. There is nobody on the

7   platform that night that we know of. If they

8   were there, they didn't make themselves known to

9   anybody either during, at the time of or after

10   the accident. We don't know. Dustin has no

11   recollection, he'll tell you, of walking into the

12   train station, of being on the platform, of being

13   on the tracks. He doesn't recall getting hit by

14   the train. You'll hear from him that in some

15   ways that's a blessing. He doesn't recall that.

16   He has no recollection of being taken out of the

17   subway station at all. So, we don't know that,

18   and we won't be able to give you the answers to

19   those questions.

20   We do know some things. We do know some

21   things from Dustin, and we have the benefit of

22   having a lot of reports generated by the police

23   and the Transit Authority as a result of the

24   accident. We were able to question the person

25   driving the train and another person on the

 2   train.

 3   Let me tell you a little bit about what

 4   we do know. We know what Dustin was wearing. He

 5   wore what he had worn into work that day, similar

 6   to what he's dressed like today. Blue jeans,

 7   brownish, tan Timberland boots. He had a black

 8   button down shirt on and he had sweatshirt on.

 9   He had a black, what they call a hoodie, a hooded

10   sweatshirt from Old Navy that said Brooklyn

11   across the front in burgundy letters. And in the

12   hood, the lining of the hood it was burgundy.

13   That's what we know about what he was wearing.

14   The station where this happened, the 14th

15   Street station, was well lit, okay. The

16   florescent bulbs were on. The station was lit

17   up. We know that the accident happened in the

18   station, on the tracks, as opposed to inside the

19   tunnel somewhere or between stations.

20   Now, you're going to get a video that we

21   took of the train's approach into the subway

22   station. You'll get an idea of what it looks at.

23   Basically what you're going to learn, members of

24   the jury, is that as the southbound local N train

25   comes into the station, it comes in the way I'm

26   showing you, as I'm walking down the jury bar

1   (indicating) here. The platform is to the left

2   of the train, where you folks are sitting in the

3   jury box. And the train comes straight down in

4   front, okay. So, as the train is heading down,

5   the platform is to the left as it enters the

6   station, and to the right there is Whitehall, all

7   right.

8   And we know that the accident happened in

9   the station, okay, and that it happened on the

10   tracks. And we know that Dustin got there

11   accidentally, all right. You're not going to

12   hear that Dustin was a jumper or he was depressed

13   or trying to commit suicide. Quite to the

14   contrary. You'll learn Dustin is a very happy

15   young man, aspiring to do lots of great things,

16   and by no means wanting to take his life, okay.

17   He ended up on the train tracks

18   accidentally, we do know that. This is not a

19   jumper case, members of the jury. You will learn

20   through evidence that will show you that he was

21   on the tracks for a significant period of time

22   before he was hit by the train. Okay. We're

23   going to show you this by introducing reports

24   into evidence from the Transit Authority as well

25   as the transcripts of some people that we

1   questioned, people on the train.

2   Now, we don't know how Dustin got on the

3   tracks. We know it was an accident. Of course

4   you're going to hear he was intoxicated. We

5   don't know for certain that that's what caused

6   him to be on the tracks. We do anticipate,

7   however, that the Transit Authority is going to

8   make quite a to do about it, that he was

9   intoxicated. I want to tell you right now, we're

10   not going to dispute that.

11   You might hear somebody come in, a

12   toxicologist or someone with lots of degrees.

13   They will tell you the types of calculations they

14   ran, say his intoxication level with percentages,

15   maybe .17 or .18. He was over the legal limit

16   they are going to say.

17   I want you to keep in mind, members of

18   the jury, he wasn't driving. So, there is no

19   legal limit for getting on a train. Secondly, in

20   our opinion, we don't think it matters, okay.

21   People end up on the tracks.

22   And you're going to hear that this

23   evening, the accident involving Dustin, it was

24   wet out. He was tired. He could have slipped.

25   He may have fallen asleep. The platform area

1   near where the accident happened is narrow. But

2   again, we're not going to get pulled into that.

3   We're not concerned about that, because we know

4   he ended up on the tracks.

5   You'll learn, members of the jury, that

6   the story doesn't stop there. That there is

7   someone who drives the train called a train

8   operator. The train operator's obligation is to

9   look for people and things on the tracks. It is

10   known that people end up on the tracks. Everyone

11   has heard about it, and you'll hear the witnesses

12   in this courtroom talk about it, most likely

13   witnesses that work for the Transit Authority.

14   They know people have ended up on the tracks,

15   sometimes by accident, sometimes not.

16   There are two people that work on subway

17   trains for the Transit Authority generally, and

18   there were two people working on the train that

19   struck Dustin. The train operator, which is also

20   in the past referred to as a motor man. That is

21   the person whose at the front of the train, that

22   you see as the train is coming into the station,

23   the person that drives the train. You'll also

24   hear there is a train conductor. That is the

25   person towards the middle of the train, that

1   drops down the window, you see when you're on the

2   platform, who looks, opens the doors, shuts the

3   doors and makes announcements, okay.

4   You're going to hear from the conductor

5   of that train, a gentleman by the name of Angel

6   V. We ask that he come here and testify as

7   to what he knew about what happened that night.

8   And, as you know from jury selection,

9   unfortunately the operator of the train will not

10   be here to testify. He's passed away since the

11   happening of the accident. So, we won't be able

12   to get his live testimony. But you're going to

13   learn generally what the obligations of an

14   operator are, what that job means. There is a

15   reason that somebody is in that position to drive

16   the train. And there is a reason that the trains

17   in New York are not automated just to go and stop

18   and move.

19   You'll learn that they are trained, they

20   are trained to see things, not just to drive the

21   train. Anybody can put a throttle on and off.

22   But to know what they are doing, to be trained

23   and experienced. You'll learn that this train

24   operator had that training and was experienced.

25   He had been doing the job many, many years. He

1   had been on this train line for many years, okay.

2   And, if anything, he should have known that on a

3   Saturday night, at the Union Square station, you

4   got to be on the lookout for things on the

5   tracks, all right.

6   Now, we have the benefit of his

7   deposition transcript, which we'll have somebody

8   read for you here, okay. So, you'll hear what he

9   had to say. We learned some things when I

10   questioned him a year ago, back in July of 2007,

11   which was almost a year after the accident, about

12   what he observed, okay, as he came into the

13   train. This is what I expect you'll hear,

14   because it's in his transcript. That is his

15   train, as he's coming into the station, you'll

16   see it wasn't some sharp turn right into the

17   station, that he was able to see for a piece of

18   time as he approach the station the actual

19   station, the lights on and the tracks. You'll

20   learn, members of the jury, that the operator of

21   the train, his name is Michael M, Mr. M.

22   That as Mr. M was operating his train, and as

23   he was approaching the station, when he was about

24   225 feet away from the front of that station, he

25   saw something on the tracks, okay.

1   He saw something, and it was still, and it was on the

2   tracks. Something we now know was Dustin, a five

3   foot ten, 90 pound man.

4   You'll hear, members of the jury, that as

5   the operator was approaching the station, he saw

6   something on the tracks, and he didn't know what

7   it was, but he saw something, and he thought it

8   was a mass. You'll hear that word used in his

9   deposition. He saw a mass on the tracks, what we

10   now know is a 190 pound mass. He didn't know

11   what it was.

12   At that point, members of the jury, it is

13   our contention he saw something, he should have

14   done something. He should have stopped the train

15   when he saw something on the tracks in the

16   station. But he didn't. He continued on into

17   the tracks. He slowed the train slightly. He

18   continued on in, not knowing what it was. And

19   you'll learn, members of the jury, that at the

20   last second before coming upon what we now know

21   as Dustin, that he saw was a person or thought he

22   saw something move on the tracks in between the

23   rails. And at that time he threw the train into

24   emergency stop, but it was too late. The train

25   went right over Dustin and continued on to travel

1   a whole car length over Dustin before coming to a

2   stop. Dustin was later found and removed out

3   from under the train, between the first and

4   second train cars, okay.

5   We'll prove to you that he should have

6   stopped the train when he saw something. He

7   should have done something. He should have

8   stopped the train. Because even if he didn't

9   know it was a man on the tracks, a young man,

10   which our contention is he should have known,

11   because you don't mistake a five foot ten, 190

12   pound man on the tracks for garbage, but even if

13   he thought it was garbage or debris on the

14   tracks, it's our contention he still should have

15   stopped the train.

16   You'll learn, members of the jury, that

17   train operators are not suppose to just hit

18   things on the tracks, even if it's not a person.

19   They are not suppose to run over garbage. There

20   is something on a train -- You'll learn a little

21   bit about trains. And we've got exhibits. And

22   we've got model trains. And you'll hear from

23   people that the front of the train, as it's

24   coming in, has a device under it called a trip

25   cock, okay. And it rides under the train in the

1   vicinity of the wheels. And if that train goes

2   over something on the rails, and it hits that

3   trip cock, and it activates it, the train will

4   automatically slam into an emergency stop, okay.

5   You will learn that trains are not

6   suppose to go over something if they think that

7   something could setoff the trip cock, okay. In

8   other words, they want to be able to stop the

9   train themselves and not have it automatically go

10   into an emergency. So, whether it's garbage or a

11   big garbage bag or debris or a person, if a train

12   operator sees something, and that something is

13   big enough on the tracks that it could cause the

14   trip cock to get hit and cause the train to go

15   into emergency, they have to stop the train. And

16   that's what should have been done in this case.

17   And it didn't happen.

18   You'll learn there is absolutely no

19   reason why he couldn't have stopped the train.

20   He should have stopped it. This wasn't between

21   stations. This wasn't rush hour. He was coming

22   into a station anyway. Everyone will know from

23   experience, trains stop all the time. There is

24   no reason -- You're not going to hear any reason

25   why he shouldn't have stopped the train. We're

2   going to prove to you that he should have

3   stopped. Not only he should have stopped, but he

4   could have stopped, members of the jury.

5   This isn't a case where a train operator

6   is saying there was something there, but I just

7   couldn't have stopped in time. It was too fast.

8   It happened too fast. I couldn't have stopped.

9   We have an engineer who is going to come here and

10   show you a stopping distance chart and trains and

11   where they can stop based on speeds. We have a

12   general idea from the deposition testimony of the

13   operator how fast he was going, 20 to 25 miles an

14   hour, somewhere around that, when he first saw

15   something on the tracks and roughly when the

16   accident happened.

17   And you'll learn that from 225 feet that

18   is more than sufficient amount of time to bring a

19   train to a stop, even if you're going at the high

20   of 25 miles an hour, according to the testimony.

21   Certainly if you're going slower, that gives you

22   even more time. And we'll prove that to you.

23   But here's the kicker, okay. You're

24   going to hear from experts. And you're going to

25   hear from our expert, and they have experts that

26   they can call if they want, engineers and believe

2   me the Transit Authority has done this, and they

3   know about stopping distances. But here's the

4   kicker. The train operator himself said he could

5   have stopped in his deposition transcript, and

6   we're going to read that for you. I asked him, I

7   said, when you first saw something on the tracks,

8   at that point you decided to stop the train,

9   could you have stopped it before hitting it. And

10   you will learn, members of the jury, that he said

11   yes, he could have stopped. Not only will we

12   prove it to you, but you'll hear it from his own

13   testimony that he could have stopped.

14   Now, as the judge said, Judge Stallman

15   said in his opening charge to you, when witnesses

16   are on the stand, you have the opportunity to

17   judge them, their credibility, their

18   believability. That's part of your role to do as

19   jurors.

20   My role as a lawyer is to try to

21   highlight in witnesses, if I think a witness is

22   not credible, through cross examination, I could

23   question them in a way that I try to highlight to

24   you folks that maybe you shouldn't believe what

25   they are saying, okay. That's part of what some

26   lawyers enjoy about cross examination.

2   Unfortunately, I will not have the

3   benefit of cross examining a live train operator,

4   Mr. M. We didn't know at the time of his

5   deposition that he wasn't going to be available.

6   And you can't cross examine a piece of paper.

7   The statements are what they are. But I want to

8   give you a head's up, okay, since I'm not going

9   to be able to point out an inconsistency to you,

10   I want to give you folks a head's up when the

11   evidence comes in to pay attention to.

12   We're going to move into evidence

13   reports, statements made by the train operator to

14   the Transit Authority around the happening of the

15   accident. And you will see that the whole time

16   there were statements made, and it was clear that

17   Dustin was on the tracks, okay. He was on the

18   row bed. He was where the rails are. He was on

19   the tracks, on the rails and/or between the

20   rails, okay. That's all over the place. You're

21   going to see it in the reports.

22   And we expect you're going to hear the

23   conductor, Mr. V, and you'll learn that he

24   and Mr. M, they knew each other. They worked

25   together for many years. They talked and they

26   knew each other. And we expect you're going to

2   hear from Mr. V said that that was the case

3   and confirm that.

4   A year after these statements were made

5   and reports were taken by the Transit Authority,

6   reports you'll see, when I questioned the train

7   operator, he tried to change his story a little

8   bit and say he didn't see someone on the tracks

9   when he first saw something. That he saw

10   something and it was kind of to the left of the

11   tracks and maybe even under the platform a little

12   bit, and that's what he said. He talked a lot

13   about, as he was approaching, it was to the left

14   and left of the tracks, not on the tracks and

15   under the platform. And I confronted him with

16   his prior statements, and he acknowledged yeah, I

17   guess I said that. Maybe they misunderstood me.

18   I want to give you that head's up.

19   You'll hear from his transcript him

20   saying that when he saw something, it was to the

21   left of the rails and it was underneath the

22   platform somewhere here. So, I want you to keep

23   an eye out, because I'm going to be highlighting

24   the evidence and all the reports that show that

25   he was on the tracks. And I challenge you and I

26   challenge the Transit Authority to show you one

2   report that says otherwise. There is nothing

3   about him under the platform or to the left of

4   the rails. I just want to give you that head's

5   up, all right.

6   Now, as he approached the station, he

7   didn't stop the train and it ran over Dustin, all

8   right. And while Dustin won't be able to tell

9   you what that felt like, you're going to hear

10   some observations of the train operator, in fact,

11   Dustin was screaming, how they had to get him out

12   and what happened. You'll hear from the train

13   conductor what happened as well.

14   You'll learn that Dustin was taken to

15   Bellevue Hospital. They have a serious trauma

16   center there. That while the train ran over his

17   right leg, the right dominant leg, that's his

18   leg, his left kicking leg, it crushed his -- the

19   lower part of his right leg, dislocated his left

20   hip. His right foot was what they called

21   traumatically amputated, hanging off of his leg,

22   still connected by the skin. He had to have

23   surgeries at the hospital. They had to go in

24   surgically, take it off.

25   He had three surgeries. One to amputate

26   it, to clean it off. More to go in and clean the

2   infection. There was a lot of debris and

3   nastiness from being on the tracks and getting

4   hit by the train. Dustin had to have a third

5   revision amputation surgery.

That surgeon will come in and testify and explain to you
what transpired in the hospital with Dustin.

8   He was at the hospital for three weeks.

9   He did rehabilitation. He went from being a

10   young, physically active man that played sports

11   every chance he could, he did pickup games,

12   pickup basketball with his friends from Bergdorf

13   Goodman. Lived the life of a fun, young, single

14   guy. How dramatically that changed.

15   You'll learn that he did everything he

16   could to try and get back to the level of where

17   he was before the accident. He was -- He worked

18   with the clinic at Bellevue. He was fitted for a

19   prosthesis. It's a device. He has a fake leg

20   from here down (gesturing) and a fake foot, okay.

21   You'll see that here. Dustin will show it to

22   you. That the stump of his leg goes into -- goes

23   into a cup, a socket and then the rest of the

24   technology goes down from there.

25   Fortunately, for Dustin, he's a healthy,

26   young, strong, athletic guy with good balance.

2   And you'll hear how he worked tirelessly to try

3   and get back to being able to do what he used to

4   be able to do. You'll probably see him

5   throughout the trial walking around. You'll see

6   him come up. He's worked very hard to get to a

7   point where people out in the street or in public

8   won't even know he has a disability, okay.

9   He's gotten to a point where he could jog

10   slowly on a treadmill. He has even walked

11   himself out to a basketball court, tried to shot

12   some hoops. He has done everything in his power

13   tirelessly through rehabilitation to get to a

14   sense of normalcy. You'll hear from Dustin how

15   he has done that.

16   You'll hear how, as much as he tried to

17   do that, he still can't run full court. He can't

18   play in a basketball game. He can't do things

19   that we all take for granted.

20   You'll hear how daily life is so impacted

21   by the loss of a limb in ways you could never

22   imagine until it happens.

23   There is a stomach bug going around,

24   where in the middle of the night he had to wake

25   up and run to the bathroom, okay, because his

26   stomach was acting up on him. You'll hear from

2   Dustin when he doesn't have a leg, if he didn't

3   have time to get to some crutches, he would

4   literally have to crawl.

5   You'll hear how simple things of his

6   daily life have been effected by this. You'll

7   hear how it has effected his social life. A

8   single guy, tried to meet women in the city and

9   go out and date. You'll hear how it's a concern

10   for him. When to bring up the subject to a woman

11   he's meeting about his leg. Whether you bring it

12   up too early, it scares him off. Whether you

13   wait too late when you try to be somewhat

14   intimate, how that could be a problem. I don't

15   need to tell you a lot about that.

16   You'll hear how his dreams have changed.

17   That he can't go and join the FBI SWAT and do

18   active types of investigation that he hoped to

19   do. He's very proud of what he's been able to

20   do. You'll see how he's been limited.

21   He's only 25 years old, members of the

22   jury. He will talk to you about how having this

23   injury at this time of his life has been so

24   difficult. He'll tell you that.

25   Members of the jury, the train operator

26   had a duty. He had an obligation to see what was

2   there to be seen on the tracks and to act. If he

3   saw something, to do something, and he didn't.

4   And we intend to prove to you that he was

5   negligent, and he's responsible for Dustin's

6   injury, regardless of how Dustin got up on the

7   track.

8   As he was approaching that station he

9   didn't say oh, well, maybe that guy is drunk. I

10   get a free pass. He doesn't get a free pass,

11   okay. Yeah, Dustin was on the track. Yeah, he

12   was intoxicated. But there was time and

13   opportunity to stop. And we'll prove to you that

14   the defendant, Transit Authority, through their

15   operator, Michael M, failed to stop the train

16   timely, and he's responsible for the horrific

17   injuries that Dustin has been left with. Thank

18   you.

19   THE COURT: Thank you, Mr. Smiley.

20   MR. SMILEY: Thank you, your Honor.

CHAPTER 3

DIRECT-EXAMINATION

This chapter explains how to properly conduct a direct-examination of a lay witness, such as a plaintiff, defendant, or witness in a personal injury case. It will give you the ability to go to court and conduct a direct-examination even if you've never done one before. And if you've conducted many direct-examinations before, you might still pick up a few tidbits.

The Value of a Smooth Direct-Examination

When I think of the word "direct," I think of it as if I'm a director, because a good direct-examination is like directing an actor or a performer in a play. You're on the stage. You have the judge and the jury in your audience. You want to present everything seamlessly and smoothly in a direct exam. And it's not easy to do without proper preparation.

If you're watching a play, TV show, or movie with good acting, you usually don't comment on it. If you're savvy, you might say, "Wow! This person is an amazing actor," but otherwise, you enjoy the show and don't think about the acting. But if you watch a show or a program with bad acting? You really notice how horrible it is.

It's the same with a direct-examination at trial. If you conduct an effective, efficient direct-examination, no one will likely say, "Wow! That was an incredible direct-examination." But suppose you do a poor direct-examination. In that case, if you're not organized, you're not prepared, you're floundering with your questions, you're disjointed, or you don't enter an item into evidence smoothly, it looks terrible to the jury, the judge, and your adversary. It's essential to prepare yourself and your witness for the direct-examination so it appears smooth and easy, even though it's not.

49

Many people get excited about cross-examination. That can be the superstar part of the trial. Lawyers have said, "I cross-examined that witness, and I took him down. Did you see that?" But nobody (except for maybe me) leaves a trial and says, "I'm so happy with that direct-examination."

Direct-examination is not sexy or exciting, and it doesn't have "a-ha" moments. But I love a good direct exam because it's where you can bring out the important parts of your case and present them in a way that will impact the jury. A strong and smooth direct-examination helps you win.

How 'Bout Them Apples?

I like to use the analogy of picking apples throughout a trial. The apples are the pieces of evidence and the important parts you need to either make a *prima facie* case as a plaintiff, or, if you're defending a case, to establish the elements of your defense. This "apple picking" starts in direct-examination and goes through cross-examination. You need to make sure that in your direct exam, you have a plan to get those apples into evidence. If you don't, they won't get to the jury.

When you are preparing for your summation, you gather all those apples, look back at your trial, and say, "Yes! I got this apple on direct of my witness. I got this apple from the direct of my expert witness. I got this apple from the cross-exam of their expert." If you do it right, by the end of the trial you will have all the apples you need to win, organize them, bake them up, and serve the delicious apple pie to the jury during your summation. You pull it all together, and you present it in a way that a jury is going to eat it up, they're going to love it, and they're going to help you win your case.

So, think about the apples you need when you're preparing and conducting a direct-examination. You must have a plan. You can't just get up there and ask questions. You need to have a reason for every question you're asking. The reason could be:

- You need to get background
- You want the jury to learn a little bit about the client
- You have to give an argument on causation, and you need to get it out of this witness

- You need to establish the damages

Solid Preparation Is the Key

If you have attended my continuing legal education (CLE) seminars, listened to The Mentor Esq. Podcast, or read my first book, *How to Successfully Litigate a Personal Injury Case*, you know that my mantra is, "Preparation, Preparation, Preparation!" That goes for yourself and your client. For a direct-examination, you're going to prepare the hell out of yourself and your witness, who is usually your client. You're going to inform your client, or your witness, about the process. You must work together like a director and an actor. You must tell them what you will ask, how you will ask it, and how you want them to present their answer. It must be a coordinated effort for the direct-examination to come out smoothly and effectively.

Prepare yourself. When I'm preparing for a trial, I look at the jury instructions and the judge's charges for the beginning of the case, the end of the case, and the facts applicable to my type of case, whether it's a construction accident, trip and fall, medical malpractice or auto accident. Is it an aggravation of a preexisting injury? What are the interesting things going on that I need to prepare for? Once I know what elements I need to establish, I sit down and write them out.

Make a plan for your witnesses. Next, I look at my witness list and decide which witnesses I want to call at which time. Usually, the first witness in an injury case is the plaintiff (although sometimes there may be strategic reasons not to have the plaintiff as the first witness). What do you want to get out of the plaintiff? You want to humanize the plaintiff and find a way to relate the plaintiff to the jury.

My father always told me that if a jury likes your client, you've got a good shot at winning the trial. And if you have an unlikable client, that's a problem. I agree wholeheartedly. Sometimes clients are likable, but they don't come across that way, or they're nervous or present themselves to a jury in a way that may not show their likability. So, you might have to work on them. For example, you might have to teach them how to smile and nod. Think about that as you develop your plan.

© 2024 Andrew J. Smiley, The Mentor Esq. All Rights Reserved

Create an outline. You want to have your outline or questions in a trial notebook, which is a binder with dividers for opening, direct, etc. Some people like a binder, and some like yellow pads. I use yellow pads a lot, and I have separate yellow pads for different examinations throughout the trial. You want to prepare in a way that's comfortable for you.

Here is a template you can follow for creating a direct-examination outline of a plaintiff:

1. Ask witness to look at jury and introduce herself

2. Give background information (extent will vary by witness/case)

    a. Residence

    b. Education

    c. Employment

    d. Age

    e. Married/single/kids/grandkids

    f. Relevant background for specific case facts

3. Turn attention to date of accident

    a. Start with the morning

    b. Chronologically lead up to the accident

4. The accident

    a. Open questions asking witness to describe—in sections—events of accident

        i. Where were you coming from/going to?

        ii. How was the weather?

        iii. What route did you take?

        iv. Did something out of the ordinary happen?

        v. What happened?

        vi. Then what?

        vii. Then what?

    b. Introduce exhibits (photos, documents, etc.)

    c. Witnesses?

    d. Statements made at the scene

e. Who responded?

f. How did you leave the scene (ambulance?)

5. Damages

    a. Medical Treatment

        i. Chronologically go through medical treatment to present time

        ii. Touch on hospitalizations, surgeries, rehab

        iii. Address pain and suffering

        iv. Did it hurt?

        v. How did you feel during rehabilitation?

    b. Current Pain and Suffering and Loss of Enjoyment questions

        i. Are you in pain now? Describe?

        ii. Have the injuries you sustained in this accident had an impact on your social life? Your employment? Your marriage? Your hobbies?

    c. Concerns for the future

        i. Future surgery

        ii. Future expenses

        iii. Future earnings

        iv. Future physical deterioration

        v. Playing with grandkids

        vi. Enjoying hobbies

6. End with "What, for you, has been the worst part about the injuries you have sustained from this accident?"

As you see in the above outline template, you start with who your client is, then bring out elements that will impact the case. In the Appendix to this chapter is the trial transcript of my direct-examination of Dustin, my client who was badly injured when he was struck by a subway train in New York City. I started his direct-examination with a focus on the fact that he was a young college athlete in his 20s. I wanted to bring out his background in sports, the teams he was on, the positions he played in college and high school, and any accolades he earned. I knew that information would make an impact later on in his testimony, when he would testify that he could no longer play sports the same way as a result of losing his foot and lower leg in the accident.

Oscar's case involved a motorcycle-car accident in Queens, New York. I tried Oscar's case one week before the pandemic shut down the country. Oscar was an avid motorcyclist, and I wanted to make sure the jury wouldn't hold that against him, since many New York City residents find motorcyclists dangerous with how they operate on the city streets. I asked questions on his direct-examination to highlight his love of riding, how he idolized his beautiful Harley-Davidson, how he only took it out for special events, and how he drove carefully. The jury liked Oscar and returned a verdict in his favor.

Finish with the impact questions. How do your client's injuries impact their life? Have they lost income? You must ask the right questions to elicit testimony (apples) regarding their pain and suffering, loss of enjoyment of life, and concerns about the future. The right question—and preparation—can result in powerful statements made by an injured plaintiff on the witness stand, such as "I will never be able to chase my grandchildren around or throw a football with them like I was hoping to."

Notes Are OK in direct-examination. You can write notes down in an outline form or type up or write out questions. This is the one time you have a chance to actually read questions. I don't like to use notes in an opening statement, a summation, or a cross-examination because I need to directly engage with the jury or the witness. But in direct-examination, you can look at your notes and your questions. So, write out specific questions for critical parts for the record that you need to make your case.

For example, when questioning a medical expert to establish causation, you must ask, "Doctor, do you have an opinion, within a reasonable degree of medical certainty, as to whether the accident was a substantial factor in causing the injury sustained by my client?" You do not want to forget to ask these critical questions, or improperly ask critical questions, so write or type them out in your outline.

Open-Ended Questions and Leading Questions
You need to be careful how you phrase your questions in a direct-examination. There are two main "types" of questions that trial attorneys ask: open-ended questions and leading questions.

- An example of an open-ended question is, "What happened next?" It is "open" because there is no way to know in advance what the answer will be by just hearing the question alone.

- An example of a leading question is, "You walked your dog that night, didn't you?" This is a leading question because you're suggesting the answer within the question and only giving the witness the opportunity to say yes or no.

Leading questions are not appropriate in direct-examination. You're not allowed to lead a witness because the questioning would go like this: "You were riding a motorcycle that day, right?" "Yes." "And this person came out and hit you out of nowhere, right?" "Yes." "And you were badly injured, right?" "Yes." It's not allowed. The information must come from the witness without your question suggesting what the answer should be.

In direct-examination, you must be careful to ask only open questions like "What happened next?" or "Tell us about this." Great open-ended questions start with who, what, where, why and when. You're opening the door for the witness to give a narrative answer instead of a yes or no. Sometimes you have something challenging to bring out without leading the witness. That's what you need to prepare with them when you practice.

For example, in my case with Oscar, I wanted to ensure that my client said he only brought his motorcycle out for charity events. But I can't say, "Do you only bring your motorcycle out for charity events?" because that's a leading question. What if I say, "When do you bring your motorcycle out?" but he forgets the charity events part and says, "Oh, I bring it out when it's a nice day." I might ask, "Are there special reasons you bring it out?" And he might say, "Oh because I love to drive it." And I'm thinking, "Come on, say the thing about the charity events." Preparation of the witness will solve this problem. Prior to trial, I spent time going over the questions I would be asking and the best way for Oscar to answer them. I told him, "When I ask you when do you bring your motorcycle out?" you must answer, "For charity events." I kept asking the same question in preparation for trial and he eventually understood what the answer should be. To be clear, I did not "coach" or "tell" Oscar what to say—that is not permissible. I knew from his deposition testimony that he would only bring his motorcycle out for special occasions like the charity event he was on his way to when the accident happened. I "prepared" him to provide that information in response to my question at trial.

Prepare your witness for a possible objection. You can also prepare a witness in case they forget how to respond to a question you ask on direct-examination. I tell my clients that if I keep asking the same question a bit differently, it means they have yet to give me the answer we need. I tell them that if all else fails, "I'll lead you. I'll get objected to, and then I'll ask an open question." So, in that situation, I might say, "Do you also bring your motorcycle out for charity events?" Your adversary will say, "Objection, leading." The judge will say, "Sustained." You can then say, "Anything else you bring your motorcycle out for?" And the witness knows to say, "Yes, charity events."

You have to be careful with open-ended and leading questions. Generally, only open-ended questions are permissible on direct-examination. Your adversary can object if it's a leading question, and it's not going to look good if you keep getting questions objected to and sustained. Plus, it can interrupt your flow. If you don't know how to ask the right question in an open format, it will break up your direct. So, make sure you know how to ask an open-ended question.

Techniques for forming open-ended questions. Sometimes you might say, "What did you say to that person?" Your adversary might object because you're suggesting they said something to that person. So, you often want to preface it by saying, "What, *if anything*, did you say? Who, *if anyone*, did you see there? When, *if at all*, did you go out that day?" Those are all phrases you can add to your questions that can turn what might be considered leading questions into proper open-ended questions.

Preparing Your Witness

Preparing your witness is crucial—I can't overstate the importance of having your client or witness prepared in advance. I often prepare a client for trial on at least two occasions, and more if necessary. I look at when the trial is expected to start, and I schedule the client for two preparation days, spaced out over a few days or a week, so they have time to digest what we discussed in the first session. Preparing helps your client feel comfortable and perform better during direct-examination. You should prepare them in advance, and you should prepare them several times.

Choose a large room. I like to meet my client in a conference room or a large office setting, so I can recreate a scenario where there's some distance between my client and me, just as there will be distance between us at the trial.

Sketch the courtroom. I show the client where the judge sits and explain that the jury box will either be on this side or on that side. I draw where the counsel tables usually are. And I say, "You're going to be sitting up here, and what's going to happen is, the judge is going to say, 'Mr. Smiley, call your first witness.' I'm going to stand up and say, 'I call the plaintiff, Mr. A., to the stand.'" And I tell my client, "When I do that, you're going to get up, walk over here to this witness stand, and here's what's going to happen. They're going to ask you to have a seat or stand, and they're going to swear you in."

Explaining all these things takes away a lot of the fear a person will naturally have at trial. Consider how you're nervous going into a courtroom, even if you've done it many times. Imagine your client, who is not a professional. It's nerve-wracking. The more you can prepare them for what's going to happen, the better.

Explain where you will be when questioning them. I always position myself at the end of the jury box. When the witness comes up, I get up from the counsel table, take my trial notebook or yellow pad, and walk to the far corner of the jury box. That is where I ask my questions from, and I highly recommend that you ask your questions from that position on direct-examination. There are important reasons for standing in that spot.

Standing there forces your witness to look towards you, which means they are looking towards the jury box. When I prepare my clients, I tell them to look at the jury when they answer. I say, "Just because I'm asking you the question, I'm asking it for the benefit of the jury. So even though I know it's kind of weird, listen to me asking, and then turn to the jury and give your answer." And I stand there, and I'll say, "Please tell the jury," and I'll gesture with my hand towards the jury.

By positioning myself at the far end of the jury box, I can remind the witness to look at the jury when answering, using a simple gesture or nod of the head. You don't want the jurors just to see a conversation between you and the witness. You want your witness to make eye contact with the jurors. Eye contact is critical for believing somebody. You want your client to look jurors in the eye and tell them the truth. And a lot of jurors will say, "That witness wouldn't even look us in the eye." So, it's important.

I also like to stand at the back end of the jury box for sound control. Some courtrooms have microphones, and some don't. Some have ones that don't work well. You want to make sure the jurors are hearing your witness. You spent all this time preparing them, and you don't want their answers to go unheard. If I'm standing at the end of the jury box and I can't clearly hear my witness's answer, I'm pretty sure that the jurors, at least the jurors closer to me, maybe jurors 6, 7, or 8 all the way to the end, are not hearing it. I'll interrupt my client or witness and say, "Can you please speak up? I'm having a hard time hearing you. I want to make sure the jury hears you."

Practice having your witness speak to the jury. When you're preparing your client in your office or your conference room, have them sit down at the end of the table, further away, imitating being on a witness stand. I stand back and go through my questions and answers with them, and I explain to them that I will say, "Mr. A., please tell the jury. Please let the jury know. Please explain. Please describe."

When I do that, I move my hands, and that's a sign to turn to the jury. I'll bring in a staff member from my office, or someone who accompanied my client or witness, and I'll ask them to sit off to the side where the jury would be. I'll ask a question and have the witness practice answering: "Can you please introduce yourself to the jury?" "Hi, my name is Oscar"

It seems simple and maybe even a little silly, but it's essential. Tell them to smile. Tell them to speak clearly. Tell them to keep their voice up and practice it. Practice asking them questions, and once they stop looking at the jury, say, "Can you please tell the jury? Please let the jury know." By the time the trial comes, they will be prepared for that.

Talk to them about what to wear. Think about how they are going to look to the jury and give them guidance on outfits. I don't want a client or witness to look like a lawyer, so I don't want a man dressed in a suit and tie or a woman dressed in a business outfit. I want them to look like who they are. I had a ski accident case where my expert witness was being deposed, and I said, "You're a skier. You're not a guy in a suit and tie. Wear what you wear with your ski gear. It will look more appropriate."

Usually, you can say, "Wear your Sunday best" or, "Wear what you would to your in-law's house for a holiday meal." Button-down shirts, sweaters, and nice clothes are appropriate. You don't want them to look overdressed or underdressed. You can ask them to dress "for court" the next time they come in to prepare, and you can let them know what you think of their outfit for court.

Advise them not to wear fancy jewelry. My father loves to tell a story about how a jury didn't award a lot of money to a client because they saw her ample diamond earrings. They thought, "Oh, she doesn't need it. She looks like she is pretty wealthy." You never know what a jury is going to look at.

In a case I tried as a young lawyer in Brooklyn, NY, my client had stepped into the gap between the platform and the subway train, and the train took off and dragged him. When he showed up to court on the day of his testimony, he wore these flat-soled, shiny dress shoes that looked like they would make you slip if you were standing still. My father looked at him and said, "He can't wear those shoes." My wife was there (she often comes to watch my trials) so she took him out to Montague Street in Brooklyn, found a shoe store, and got him some rubber-soled, normal-looking shoes, because you never know what a jury is going to see. Appearances matter, especially on direct-examination.

Review the entire direct-examination with your witness. Have your outline ready before the client or witness arrives for preparation. Don't just wing it. Ask them the questions and go through the outline. Maybe you do half of it on the first meeting, then give them a sample of your outline or questions and tell them, "Go home and practice. Let your spouse ask you the questions, and you practice answering." There's nothing wrong with that. You're not telling them what to say. You're asking them to practice answering questions out loud, so they feel comfortable.

If it's a wrongful-death claim, I might say, "Listen, at trial, I have to ask you about the impact the loss of your husband has had on your young children." I'll ask them to think about what they want to say to the jury and be prepared to say it. I'll prepare them to not be afraid to cry. To let the jury feel their emotion. Those are important things. You must give your witness the freedom to provide answers in a compelling way and let them know that you want them to do that.

Explain the concept of redirect-examination. I tell clients what cross-examination is and how to prepare for it. I ask them to read their pretrial deposition transcript thoroughly, and I explain how impeachment works. You want to prepare and inform your client and witness so they're not like a deer in headlights. Prepare them to answer questions on cross-examination with respectful, short, and direct responses.

Let them know they might be asked a leading question on cross-examination and feel like they're not allowed to fully answer it. The lawyer might cut them off and keep going, or something might come out that they haven't had a chance to explain. Let them know that's what redirect-examination is for. For example, I will have the opportunity to get up and say, "Now, Mr. A., defense counsel didn't let you give an answer as to why you didn't look in your sideview mirror at that moment. Can you explain to the jury why you didn't look in your sideview mirror?" And then Mr. A. can say, "Yes. I just looked two seconds ago, and there was no car for 200 feet back, so I didn't think I had to look again." Whatever it may be, explain the redirect process. That's as important in your preparation of the witness as everything else.

Go through the items you want to introduce into evidence. Many times, for the plaintiff, you're going to introduce photographs of the accident scene, photographs of injuries, and documents they have received or prepared. If you have a medical witness, you need to introduce medical records or exhibits or enlargements. You need to think about that when you're planning the direct-examination of witnesses, because it's not just going to be testimonial evidence. There will be photos, documents, videos, tax returns, or other "apples" you want to put into evidence.

In my firm, when we are preparing for a trial, we will ask, "How are we going to get this into evidence? Which witness should we use? How will it be most effective?" You want to go over the items with the witness in advance. If it's the plaintiff in an injury case, you want to go through the exhibits, photographs, accident scene, and the vehicle or the motorcycle.

In preparing Oscar for trial, I advised him, "At some point, I'm going to introduce these five photographs and ask you some questions about them. Here's one of your motorcycle. Here's another, of the intersection. Here's another that shows you on a gurney outside the ambulance. I'm going to ask the judge some things, I'm going to approach you, I'm going to show it to you, and I'm going to ask you a bunch of questions. I'm going to tell you what those questions are. Don't worry if you forget because your answer to these questions should always be 'yes.' I'm going to say, 'Oscar, does this photograph fairly and accurately depict what your motorcycle looked like on the day of the accident?" 'Yes.' Then I'm going to ask follow-up questions about the photograph—just answer 'yes.'"

Explain the process. If you're going to ask them to mark a photograph or a document, let them know. You might use a computer or projector to put an image on a screen. I'm old school, so I like to use enlarged exhibits and put them on an easel, whether it's a photograph, business record, or transcript page. The jury can look at it, I can hold it up in summation, and they can take it into the jury room. Whatever you use, walk through it. If you're going to have your witness mark things or point at things, go through that with them during the preparation.

Prepare them for signals. I like to have some signals and cues with my clients and my witness. And one of the things I use is the pen or pencil trick. I tell them in preparation or even in depositions, "Don't be too long-winded." I'll say, "If you see me hold my pen vertically on the table, it means you are talking too much. You need to tighten up your answers and make the lawyer ask you another question." If that comes up, they are saying more than they need to, and I let them know that. When you prepare them, you tell them that you will be able to get back up and redirect. They will have the opportunity to explain.

How to Enter Photographs and Documents into Evidence

It's crucial that you know how to properly enter an item into evidence. There was a time when my father was trying a case. I was observing while still in law school. The defense wanted to put a surveillance video of our client into evidence. He was a partner at a well-known firm, but he couldn't lay the proper foundation questions through his witness. My father would stand up, say, "Objection!" and look at the judge. The judge said, "Sustained. Ask another question." And

61

this went on 10 or 15 times. All my father had to do was stand up and say, "Objection," and the judge said, "Sustained."

The lawyer was flailing around, and we were all sitting there, and the jury was looking at him. It was awful. And it was because he missed one of the foundation questions of how to put something into evidence. Everything went downhill for him from there. So, asking the questions properly is important as part of the seamless presentation you're putting on for the jury. It needs to be smooth and choreographed.

The template for entering items into evidence. When I enter something into evidence, the sequence goes like this:

"Your Honor, may I approach to have this item marked for identification?"

Usually, the judge will say, "Yes, but please show it to your adversary first."

I'll say, "Yes, Your Honor" and show it to my adversary, saying, "Let the record reflect that I'm showing this document to my adversary."

The judge then says, "You may approach."

I approach in a deliberate manner, buttoned up, looking professional, and hand it to the court officer or the court clerk and say, "Your Honor, may we please have this marked as Plaintiff Exhibit 1 for identification." And the judge will say something like, " So marked as Plaintiff 1 for Identification."

Sometimes you can combine your questions and ask to have it marked at the beginning:

"Your Honor, may I approach with what I'd like to have marked as Plaintiff Exhibit 1 for identification?"

The judge will say, "Show it to your adversary."

I'll say, "Let the record reflect I'm showing what has been marked as Plaintiff Exhibit 1 for identification to counsel. May I approach?"

"Yes."

You approach and say, "And may I please approach the witness?"

"Yes."

You approach the witness and hand them the document or show it to them. If it's a blow-up, or something large, you position yourself with your back to the jury. The jury is not permitted to see an item until it is in evidence. So, there's a little cloak-and-dagger here. You're showing it, but until it's in evidence, they can't see it. Don't start waving something around on your walk up for a jury to look at it—that will get you into trouble, so keep it away from the jury. You show it to the witness while you ask the foundation questions.

Pre-marked exhibits. In Federal Court, though not in many state courts, you might be using pre-marked exhibits. With pre-marked exhibits, you sit down with your adversary and agree on all the exhibits you both plan on introducing, and you mark them. If I have 15 photographs and other documents, I label them 1 through 15. The defense could label theirs A through G. Then you have a document that has been pre-marked—it's typed up, and everybody knows what it is. You can give the court a sheet of the pre-marking, and you don't have to mark it at the time. If it gets into evidence, you can leave it as that marking. You skip the whole routine of approaching to have something marked.

Laying the foundation through your witness. Either way, you get to the point where you're approaching the witness with it and asking the judge if you may show it to the witness. And you wait for permission. You show it to the witness, and the jury cannot see it then.

Here's where I would say to my client, "Oscar, I'm handing you what has been marked as Plaintiff Exhibit 1 for identification. Do you recognize it?" I prepared him, so he says, "Yes, I do."

The next question is, "What do you recognize it to be?" And he says, "I recognize it to be a photograph of my motorcycle." Again, I have prepared him for that answer. The next question is, "And does this exhibit that I've just handed you fairly and accurately depict the motorcycle you were operating at the time of your accident?" This is the step the lawyer was missing in the case where he couldn't get the video into evidence. He didn't say, "Does this video fairly and accurately depict the video surveillance footage that you took of the plaintiff on March 10, 2009?" He kept missing this part, so he wasn't laying the proper foundation.

You need to prepare your client. If it's a photograph, a letter, or another document, you have to ask, "Does it fairly and accurately depict it?" You've prepared your client to say yes to all of your foundation questions.

Sometimes it may be a business record you're getting in through a witness. So, you may want to say, "Was this document prepared by the police department in the ordinary course of business?" "Yes, it was." You can establish the foundation that way.

For your last question, you ask, "Will this photo (or document, record, or Plaintiff Exhibit 1 for identification) aid and assist you in your testimony to this jury today?" "Yes." At that point, you stop. You turn to the judge and say, "Your Honor, we now offer what has been marked as Plaintiff 1 for identification into evidence as Plaintiff 1 (or just into evidence)." Then the judge will turn to your adversary and say, "Mr. Adversary, any objection to this?"

Potential objections. If your adversary has an objection, this is when it comes in, and you address it. If you've done it right, given notice to your adversary, and disclosed this photograph as part of your pre-trial disclosure, you won't get that objection saying, "Your Honor, I've never seen this photograph before." If you do, the judge will say, "Mr. Smiley, did you give this photograph to defense counsel prior to just now?" You'll reply, "Yes, Your Honor. In fact, here is my pre-trial disclosure. I gave it to him, and I have an affidavit of service from six months ago."

Once you get through any objection, the judge will say, "We will now receive that into evidence as Plaintiff 1. Please proceed and let the court reporter put a sticker on it." The court reporter puts a sticker on it, dates it, and identifies it as Plaintiff 1. Now it's Plaintiff 1 in evidence, and you are free to show it to the jury. You can say, "Your Honor, may I now publish this to the jury?" The judge will say something like, "Yes, of course, Mr. Smiley."

But you're showing a smooth process of how to get something into evidence. The jury, your adversary, and the judge see you and respect you as a competent attorney. That's what you want. It's the good acting part. Bad acting is when someone doesn't know how to do this, doesn't ask the proper foundation questions, and can't get a surveillance video into evidence. The jury is sitting there rolling their eyes, and the plaintiff's counsel is enjoying every minute of it. You don't want that to happen.

You don't have to use the exact words I have stated to lay a foundation, but those steps should be the gist of it. Identify it, depict it, and make sure the witness says it is fair and accurate. You use the same foundation questions to get in photographs, documents, and videos. It is essential that you do that. Practice it with your client in preparation, so that when it happens, they're not sitting there wondering why you're handing them something and what they should say.

Use the Documents You've Entered to Your Advantage

Once you get a document into evidence, use it. There's a reason that you wanted to put something into evidence. I've had a case where my client sustained bad scarring in a sensitive area, and I didn't want them to have to drop their drawers in a courtroom, so we had a photograph. And then I said, "Can we publish it to the jury?" And you hand it to them, and they can pass it around and look at it.

Sometimes you want the jury to see the smoking gun. You want them to see the evidence. You want them to see the document with the statement where your adversary's witness gave it all up, whatever it is. You want to publish it to the jury, which means you hand it to the court officer. They hand it to juror #1, they look at it, pass it around to everybody, and hand it back.

Sometimes you want to put the exhibit on an easel and have the witness come down and mark it. There are ways to do that properly. Stand to the side—don't block the jury. Put whatever you want to have your witness go through on the easel and have your markers or laser pointer ready. Tell your witness in advance, "When I bring you to the exhibit on the easel, I will guide you and tell you to mark an X where this happens or put an arrow where that happens."

Make Sure Actions Are Entered into the Record

In your direct, you have to make the record clear. If someone is marking an exhibit with a red pen, there's nothing for a court reporter to take down. You need to preserve your record. So, every time they make a note, you say, "Your Honor, may the record reflect that the witness has just placed a red X on the spot to represent where he was at the moment he was struck by the defendant's vehicle."

65

By putting it into words, if the jury asks for a read-back or, if needed for appellate review, you have it there. If you don't do that, it's not reflected. I've had a lot of trials where my adversary asks my client to mark something on cross-examination, and they don't ask for the record to reflect the marking. I'll jump in and say, "Your Honor, I'm sorry. Can we please have the record reflect that the witness has placed a red X to indicate where the vehicle struck him," or "Can we please ask counsel to have the record reflect?" You always want to protect your record. If it doesn't show up on a transcript, it didn't happen in your trial as far as any appellate review is concerned.

End Your Direct-Examination with Strength

After you've made your smooth, orchestrated presentation and you're done with everything, you end on a strong question. Make sure you know what your last question is. Have it written out and notated. If it's a damages question, or if you're at the end of a trial where damages are an issue, I like to ask, "Mr. D., what's the worst part about this injury if you can share that with the jury, please?" I like to ask, "What's the worst part," "Do you have any concerns for the future," or "What's your biggest fear looking ahead," things like that, because you're ending on a compelling question and it's open, so it's not going to be objected to.

On direct and cross-examination, you never want to end your questioning with an objection being sustained. In that case, you're effectively saying, "Oh, OK," meekly dropping your head, and walking back to your counsel's seat. You want everything you do in a trial to be strong. That's why you look everyone in the eye and walk tall back to your seat. That's why, at the end of a direct-examination, you want to end with a question, say thank you to your witness, close up your book and walk back strongly to your table.

66

CHAPTER 3 APPENDIX

MY DIRECT EXAMINATION OF DUSTIN

9   DIRECT EXAMINATION

10   BY MR. SMILEY:

11   Q.   Good afternoon, Dustin.

12   A.   Good morning.

13   Q.   Could you tell the jury how old you are.

14   A.   I'm 25 years old.

15   Q.   And when were you born? What's your date

16   of birth?

17   A.   I was born September 15th, 1983.

18   Q.   Where did you grow up?

19   A.   I grew up in a small town outside of

20   Buffalo called Corfu, New York.

21   Q.   And tell us about your family.

22   A.   My mom and my dad, my mom is right there

23   (indicating), and I have two older brothers.

24   Q.   And for how long did you stay in Corfu

25   before coming down to the city?

26   A.   I lived there my whole life, since I was

2   born.

3   Q.   And what are your brothers' names?

4   A.   My oldest brother's name is Christian,

5   and my other brother's name is Nicholas.

6   Q.   How old are they?

7   A.   Nick is 30 and Chris is 33.

8   Q.   What about your parents, what are their

9   names?

10   A.   My mom's name is Susan and my father's

11   name is Douglas.

12   Q.   What do your parents do for a living?

13   A.   My mom is a teacher, special education

14   teacher, and my dad works in construction.

15   Q.   Now, did you go to high school in Corfu

16   where you grew up?

17   A.   The high schools were located in that

18   town, but the school district was known as Pembroke.

19   Q.   Did you play any sports while in high

20   school?

21   A.   Yeah. I played throughout my entire

22   time, from 7th grade up until 12th grade. I played

23   football, basketball and baseball.

24   Q.   What positions did you play?

25   A.   Football, I played both offense and

26   defense. I was a safety on defense and wide receiver

2   on offense. I was also the punter and the kicker. In

3   terms of basketball, I played shooting guard. And

4   baseball I played center field.

5   Q.   And are you right handed dominant or left

6   hand dominant?

7   A.   Right handed.

8   Q.   What about with your legs, before your

9   accident, which was your dominant leg?

10   A.   Same thing, right. It was my right leg.

11   Q.   In high school did you receive any honors

12   either in academics or sports or anything else?

13   A.   My senior year I made all league for both

14   basketball, football and baseball. And I also made

15   the all greater Rochester basketball team, known as

16   the Ronald McDonald team. And I was voted by my peers

17   as most athletic in our senior class and also, like

18   you mentioned before, outstanding male athlete of the

19   year voted by faculty and coaching staff.

20   Q.   After graduating from high school, did

21   you go to college?

22   A.   Yes, I did.

23   Q.   Where did you go to school?

24   A.   I went to Utica College.

25   Q.   And just give the jury a general idea

26   about what type of school that is.

2   A.   It's located right in the city of Utica,

3   New York. At the time that I started attending, it

4   was affiliated with Syracuse University. When I

5   graduated, I got a Syracuse diploma. It's a small,

6   private college, maybe about -- I think at the time

7   that I enrolled it was about 2,000 was the amount of

8   people that were going there at the time. On campus

9   housing and just a typical college.

10   Q.   And did you play sports in college at

11   Utica?

12   A.   Yeah. I was recruited to play football

13   there. And while I was there for football, I actually

14   submitted one of my tapes that I made myself to the

15   basketball coach and asked him if I could try out for

16   the team. I ended up playing football freshman year

17   and left the team because I wanted to play basketball.

18   And I wasn't able to do both at the same time.

19   Q.   Did you play the same positions in

20   college that you told us about in high school?

21   A.   Yes, I did.

22   Q.   And did you graduate from Utica College?

23   A.   Yes.

24   Q.   Did you graduate with a degree?

25   A.   Yes. I graduated with a Bachelor of

26   Science degree, cuma laude.

 2   Q.   What does cuma laude mean?

 3   A.   I believe it's a GPA, overall GPA of 3.4

 4   or higher.

 5   Q.   And did you have a degree in a specific

 6   area of study?

 7   A.   The degree that I received was in

 8   economic crime investigation, criminal justice, with a

 9   concentration in computer security.

10   Q.   Is there a reason that you focused in

11   that area of study while in college?

12   A.   One of the reasons I picked that college,

13   not only because I was recruited, but the economic

14   crime investigation program, at the time Utica was one

15   of the only two colleges in the country that offered

16   that program. And from what I had talked about with

17   professors and orientation, it was high in demand in

18   terms of that field.

19   Q.   And at the time that you got your studies

20   going in that area, did you have any idea of what you

21   wanted to use that degree for? What type of work you

22   wanted to get into?

23   A.   I always had a desire to be in some type

24   of law enforcement, whether or not it had been state

25   trooper, border patrol or, you know, I was younger, I

26   talked about possibly getting into the FBI someday.

2   Q.   When you graduated from college, when was

3   that?

4   A.   Graduated in May of 2005.

5   Q.   What did you do after graduation?

6   A.   After graduation part of our requirements

7   for my major was I had to complete a ten week

8   internship. And I ended up getting an internship at

9   HIP Health Plans. It was located in Woodbridge, New

10   Jersey.

16   Q.   Can you give the jury an idea of what

17   that internship involved and what you did?

18   A.   Sure. The internship was in their

19   special investigations unit. Their main function

20   there is to focus on finding any health care fraud

21   committed against the company. And, unfortunately,

22   since I was just an intern, I was only allowed limited

23   access to the system. So, my primary obligations were

24   just to assist the other investigators in any type of

25   basic paperwork or questioning that it involved and

26   also answering their hotline to take complaints from
2   subscribers and providers.

3   Q.   Did you eventually get a paying job in

4   the field of investigation?

5   A.   Yes, I did.

6   Q.   What was your first paying job?

7   A.   My first paying job was at Bergdorf

8   Goodman as a loss prevention specialist.

9   Q.   When did you start there?

10   A.   I started there February 6, 2006.

11   Q.   At the time that you started working at

12   Bergdorf, where did you live?

13   A.   When I first started working there, I

14   lived on Staten Island, New York.

15   Q.   Did you live with anybody?

16   A.   Yes. I lived with my brother.

17   Q.   Your brother Nick who is here?

18   A.   My brother Nick, yes.

19   Q.   And what did you do for Bergdorf Goodman?

20 What was your duties there?

21   A.   I was a loss prevention specialist. We

22 were in charge of maintaining any type of integrity.

23 And we were responsible for all the merchandise and

24 the employees in the store. Also looking for

25 shoplifters, whether it was an employee or a customer.

26 Also, you know, bag checks, ID checks and any type of
 2   accidents or credit card fraud that had happened at

 3 the company.

 4   Q.   And what days of the week would you work

 5 back then, in February into April of 2006 at Bergdorf?

 6   A.   It varied. The store is a retail store.

 7 So, the only time it was closed was major holidays.

 8 We were open seven days a week. I never had steady

 9 hours in terms of the actual days. It varied from

10 week to week.

11   MR. SMILEY: Your Honor, if it's okay

12   with the Court, I think at this time it would be

13   an appropriate time to perhaps take a break. The

14   next area that we'll explore testimony will start

15   getting into the actual day of the incident.

16   THE COURT: And we would run over then.

17   MR. SMILEY: Yes. I believe we would run

18   over that time.

19   THE COURT: Okay. Very well. All right.

20   Mr. Dibble, why don't you resume your seat and

21   we'll continue your testimony tomorrow. Thank

22   you, sir.

6   CONTINUING DIRECT EXAMINATION

7   BY MR. SMILEY:

8   MR. SMILEY: May I proceed, your Honor?

9   THE COURT: You may.

10   MR. SMILEY: Thank you.

11   Q   Good morning, Dustin.

12   A   Good morning.

13   Q   We're going to pick up where we left off,

14   which is talking about your work at Bergdorf Goodman

15   and that you were working Saturday, April 22, 2006?

16   A   Yes, I was.

17   Q   Okay. Tell us, what happened towards the

18   end of that day of work.

19   A   Saturday, the store usually closes at 7,

20   and we leave anywhere in between 7:30, 8 o'clock,

21   depending on how long it takes the associates to get

22   out of the store, the customers and for us to do our

23   closing procedures.

24   And so we were just closing up the

25   store at that time and waiting to leave for the day.

26   Q   And did you have any plans or did you make

2   any plans to go out upon finishing work on Saturday?

3   A   Yes, I did.

4   Q   What did you do?

5   A   I received a call from one of my friends

6   that I've been friends with for a long time since I was

7   younger, and she said that she was up at a bar with

8   some of her friends and she asked if I wanted to meet

9   her there.

10   Q   What is this friend's name?

11   A   Her name is Nikki.

12   Q   How did you know Nikki?

13   A   I've known her since I was in sixth grade,

14   we've been friends for a long time, and we even dated

15   for a couple of years.

16   Q   And did you, in fact, go up and meet with

17   Nikki and some other people?

18   A   Yes, I did.

19   Q   And where did you go?

20   A   We went to a bar up on the Upper West Side

21   of Manhattan.

22   Q   Was that your first time going out on a

23   Saturday night in Manhattan?

24   A   No, it wasn't.

25   Q   Can you give the jury an idea of what your

26   habits were back then as far as when and where you

2   would go out in the city?

3   A   Like I said before, the days I would work

4   usually varied. Sometimes I had to work on Saturday,

5   sometimes I wouldn't. So it depends, I mean we usually

6   try to stay in the area.

7   So at the time I didn't really know

8   that many people up there, really only knew the people

9   that I worked with.

10   So when we went out, we usually

11   generally stayed just in the area where Bergdorf was

12   located.

13   Q   Where was that?

14   A   It's on 57th and Fifth Avenue.

15   Q   And were there certain nights of the week

16   that you would typically go out or not go out?

17   A   Just on the weekend, usually, I mean, the

18   days I'd have off during the week I'd used to run my

19   errands or do whatever stuff I couldn't take care of

20   because I wouldn't get out of work until, during the

21   week until 8:30, 9 o'clock, so I wasn't able to take

22   care of any errands, laundry or pay my bills, anything

23   like that that needs to take care of.

24   Q   Approximately what time did you arrive at

25   the bar when you met up with Nikki and her friends?

26   A   Approximately 9 o'clock, 9 p.m.

2   Q   Tell the jury what happened when you got

3   there, what transpired.

4   A   Well, when I got there, she'd already been

5   there with a group of friends. I wasn't aware of any

6   of the friends, I didn't know them at all, they were

7   friends I believe she met when she was at college, and

8   we met up there.

9   And when I entered, they were sitting

10   at the back at a big table. There was a group of them.

11   I went to the back and sat down and just started

12   talking.

13   Q   And were you guys drinking at the bar?

14   A   Yes, we were.

15   Q   What were you drinking?

16   A   We had pitchers of beer because there was

17   so many of people that they just ordered pitchers.

18   Q   And what transpired throughout the rest of

19   your stay at that first bar?

20   A   I just caught up with Nikki, I hadn't seen

21   her in a while, so we just reminisced, caught up on

22   things, just talked about old times and just drank.

23   Q   Can you give the jury an idea of how long

24   you were at that bar before leaving that bar?

25   A   We were there maybe an hour or two.

26   Q   And over the course of that time, about

2   how much had you drank?

3   A   Probably about three or four glasses, just

4   the typical bar glass. I don't know exactly how many

5   ounces those are, but just the typical glass you get

6   when you're out at a bar.

7   Q   You were filling that with the pitchers

8   that were at the table?

9   A   That is correct.

10   Q   And where did you go upon leaving that

11   bar?

12   A   After we left that bar, we walked, I don't

13   know how many blocks, couple of blocks, it was within

14   walking distance to a second bar.

15   Q   Okay. And do you remember what the

16   weather was that night?

17   A   It was raining out that night.

18   Q   And who was it that left the first bar

19   from the group of people that were there to go on the

20   second bar?

21   A   When we left the first bar, the only

22   people that went to the next one was me, Nikki and one

23   of her friends.

24   Q   And what did you do when you got to the

25   second bar?

26   A   When we got to the second bar, the Buffalo

2   Sabers game was on, hockey game, and so we were just

3   watching the game and just continued to talk and have a

4   couple more drinks.

5   Q   Did you have a table, like at the first

6   bar?

7   A   No, the bar is pretty busy, so there

8   wasn't any available seats to sit down, so we stood the

9   whole time.

10   Q   And did you have more beer at this bar?

11   A   Yes, we did.

12   Q   Give the jury an idea of how much you

13   drank when you were at this bar?

14   A   Usually about three or four more bottles,

15   we had bottles at the second bar.

16   Q   This amount of beer that you had, was this

17   something unusual for you or different from you as far

18   as prior nights going out for drinks?

19   A   No. I mean, I never sat there and kept an

20   exact count of, you know, how many exact glasses or

21   bottles I had drank. But just a typical night out, I

22   mean we were there for probably a total of four or five

23   hours throughout the night, so it was just constant

24   throughout the night. It wasn't anything out of the

25   ordinary.

5   Q   And from the time you left work up until

6   the end of your stay at the second bar, did you have

7   anything to eat, any type of dinner?

8   A   No, I didn't eat anything during that

9   time.

10   Q   Can you give the jury an idea of your

11   drinking habits at that time, whether or not you had

12   drank beer before when you drank in college, whether or

13   not you drank any type of alcohol?

14   A   Well, I had just graduated from college

15   maybe in May of 2005, so less than a year before I was

16   out there, I mean I was in college. I had a suite with

17   five other guys, we did what you do when you are in

18   college. We had parties, we drank and just the usual,

19   usual habits, you know, drank socially on the weekends

20   and you know, it wasn't any, anything out of the

21   ordinary for me to go out on a Saturday night after

22   work and have some drinks with some friends.

23   Q   Back at this time in April of 2006, were

24   you about the same size that you are now?

25   A   Yes.

26   Q   Okay. And how tall are you?

2   A   I'm five ten.

3   Q   And how much do you weigh?

4   A   One hundred ninety pounds.

5   Q   Now, what happened at the conclusion of

6   your stay at the second bar?

7   A   After we left the second bar, we needed

8   to, I needed to go home at the time, I was on Staten

       9   Island, so we hailed a taxi and we took a taxi to the

      10   train station.

      11   Q   Was it still raining out at that time?

      12   A   Yes, it was.

      13   Q   And who got into the taxi?

      14   A   It was me, Nikki and her friend still was

      15   at the time.

      16   Q   Do you remember her friend's name?

      17   A   No. I've been told it since, but I don't

      18   really remember it off the top of my head, no.

      19   Q   Does Anthony sound familiar?

      20   A   Yes.

      21   Q   And is there a reason that you didn't stay

      22   in the cab and take the cab home to Staten Island?

      23   A   Well, at the time I had just started that

      24   job maybe a month or two before, and I mean, when I got

      25   the job I had pretty much no money, and I had just

      26   actually got a new apartment a couple of days before

       2   that night of the accident and I had to put a down

       3   payment and first month's rent.

       4   So, at the time I wasn't, I was kind

       5   of strapped for money and through my experience from

       6   taking cabs home from Bergdorf after late nights like

       7   overtime at work, the cab rides around that area

       8   usually are around 60, 70 dollars, not including tip

9   all the way to where I lived in Staten Island.

10   So I just, I didn't have that kind of

11   money on me at the time to be able to spend on that.

12   Q   What about Nikki and Anthony, do you know

13   if they had plans to take a cab to wherever they were

14   going home?

15   A   They lived in New Jersey at the time. I

16   don't know where he lived. I knew she lived in

17   Weehawken, New Jersey, so, the only mode they were able

18   to get, they intended to take the Path train back to

19   New Jersey.

20   Q   And where did you take the cab to?

21   A   To Union Square.

22   Q   And what happened when you arrived at

23   Union Square?

24   A   We got out of the cab and said our

25   goodbyes.

26   Q   Do you know what time it was about the

2   time that you either left the bar or got in the cab or

3   got out of the cab?

4   A   I wasn't really keeping track of the time.

5   I don't remember any specific time, ever really

6   noticing any time.

7   Q   And when you arrived at Union Square, was

8   it still raining out?

9   A   Yes, it was.

10   Q   And do you recall getting out of the cab

11   and saying goodbye to Nikki and her friend?

12   A   Yes.

13   Q   Okay. And do you recall how you felt at

14   that time in view of the fact you'd been drinking all

15   night? Did you feel drunk, very drunk, did you feel

16   controlled, how did you feel?

17   A   I mean, like I said before, it wasn't any

18   night that was out of the ordinary. I felt I was in

19   control, I knew where I needed to go. I knew that I

20   had to get the train down to the Staten Island Ferry,

21   take the ferry over, which is a process in itself, and

22   from there I'd have to either take a local bus or take

23   a cab service to my house from there, I couldn't walk

24   or anything.

25   Q   Other than the method you just described

26   to get home, did you have any other way of getting home

2   that night?

3   A   Other than what we said before about maybe

4   taking a taxi all the way there, which was at the time

5   pretty expensive for me, I didn't know of any other way

6   I could have gotten back on Staten Island.

7   Q   What's the next thing you recall, Dustin,

8   after getting out of the cab and saying goodbye to

9   Nikki and her friend?

10   A   After I got out of the cab, we said our

11   goodbyes. The next thing I remember is waking up in

12   the hospital.

13   Q   And what do you recall about waking up in

14   the hospital?

15   A   This guy was, they were holding me down,

16   it was a group of people and they, the guy was holding

17   me, they needed to pop my hip back into place, it had

18   been dislocated.

19   Q   Do you have any recollection whatsoever

20   about this train accident, Dustin?

21   A   No, I don't.

22   Q   Do you remember being in the station or

23   going to the station?

24   A   No.

25   Q   Do you remember being on the platform at

26   any time?

2   A   No.

3   Q   Do you have any recollection about being

4   on the tracks or how you may have gotten on the tracks?

5   A   No, no, I don't.

6   Q   What about anything to do so with actually

7   being struck by the train?

8   A   I don't remember anything in terms of the

9   actual accident. Like I said, I got out of the cab,

10   said our goodbyes and the next thing I knew I was in

11   the hospital.

12   Q   What were you wearing on the night of the

13   accident?

14   A   I was wearing blue jeans, black shirt,

15   black sweatshirt, it was a down sweatshirt and

16   Timberland boots.

17   Q   And can you describe what the sweatshirt

18   looked like?

19   A   It was a regular like cotton sweatshirt,

20   it was a silver zipper down the front, had a hood, the

21   inside of the hood was lined with maroon and on the

22   front it said "Brooklyn" across the front in a maroon,

23   the same color maroon with white stitching around the

24   block lettering.

25   Q   Do you remember what company that was from

26   or where you got that?

2   A   I believe it was from Old Navy.

3   Q   Do you still have that sweatshirt?

4   A   No, I don't.

5   Q   And at my request did you dress today in a

6   similar fashion other than the sweatshirt as to how you

7   were dressed on the evening of the accident?

8   A   Yes, I am.

9   Q   And what you're currently wearing, just so

10   we know for the record, what are you wearing?

11   A   I'm wearing a dark colored shirt, button

12   down, blue jeans and Timberland boots.

13   Q   What color are the Timberland boots that

14   you are wearing?

15   A   They're tan and with black sole bottoms.

16   Q   And were you wearing similar boots on the

17   night of the accident?

18   A   Yes.

19   Q   And similar jeans on the night of the

20   accident?

21   A   Yes.

22   Q   Now, we expect there to be some evidence

23   or testimony that you were observed at some point on

24   the tracks and what's been described as a Muslim

25   praying, someone down on their knees with their

26   buttocks in the air, leaning forwards.

2   MR. SMILEY: And with the Court's permission,

3   we'd ask that Dustin be able to come down into the well

4   of the courtroom to get into that Muslim prayer for

5   purposes of demonstrating to the jury how he may have

6   appeared on that night.

7   THE COURT: All right.

8   MR. GIORDANO: No objection.

9   Q   Dustin, could you come down here, please.

10   Take your time.

11   (The witness leaves the stand.)

12   Q   Now what I'd like you to do, so the jury

13   could see, take your time, get slowly down with your

14   head facing this way. This way, okay? On your knees,

15   and rest down on your arms, if you can. Okay.

16   MR. SMILEY: If the jury wants to take a

17   moment just to look to see that.

18   THE COURT: Okay.

19   MR. SMILEY: Everyone has had a moment.

20   Q   All right, Dustin, thanks. You can get up

21   now.

22   (The witness resumes the stand.)

23   Q   Now Dustin, I want to pick up where we

24   left off at the hospital, okay?

25   By the way, before we get to the

26   hospital, were you ever told by anybody there were any

2   witnesses to your accident?

3   A   No, I wasn't aware of any. I wasn't told

4   that there was any witnesses to what happened.

5   Q   And as far you know, no one was going with

6   you into the train, right?

7   A   I didn't have any plans to meet anyone at

8   the train station, anything like that, so no, there is

9   no reason that I know of that anyone would have been

10   with me.

11   Q   As best as you can, tell the jury about

12   what you recall about the initial phase of your stay at

13   the hospital.

14   A   Well, like I said, first I remember, I had

15   my hip popped back into place and then --

16   Q   Which hip was that?

17   A   It was my left. My left hip.

18   And the initial thing that had to

19   happen was the amputation was the first surgery and

20   then while I was there, my initial stay was -- I'd had

21   to have multiple surgeries, because in terms of the

22   sanitary conditions of the tracks, and the way it was,

23   they were concerned with any type of infection. I was

24   running a little bit of a fever, they didn't establish

25   any type of infection, but they were concerned that

26   something could develop.

2   So, they took a lot of precautions to

3   go in there and continually clean out the leg and make

4   sure at no time there was a chance that I could develop

5   any infection.

6   Q   By the way, what hospital was this?

7   A   This is Bellevue Hospital on First Avenue.

8   Q   Now, you said the dislocation of the hip

```
 9    was your left hip, which part was amputated of your

10    body?

11          A      The lower half of my right leg.

12          Q      And do you know from what point of your

13    right leg the initial surgery for the amputation was

14    performed, where that was done?

15          A      I don't know exactly where.  I know right

16    now it's about halfway between where my ankle would be

17    and my knee, so about halfway down your shin.

18          Q      And you said there were a few surgeries

19    that focused just on that area of the amputation?

20          A      Yes.

21          Q      Do you recall the moment when you first

22    learned that you had lost your leg and had been in a

23    train accident?

24          A      Yeah, I do.

25          Q      Tell the jury about that.

26          A      Kind of coming to a little bit and my mom

 2    was standing there, and you know, I could tell by the

 3    look on her face that something wasn't right and she

 4    just said that they had to amputate my -- the lower

 5    half of my right leg.

 6          Q      How did you feel when you heard that for

 7    the first time?

 8          A      I didn't feel good.
```

9   Q   Do you know how you reacted upon hearing

10   the news?

11   A   Disbelief. You know, kind of saying,

12   something kind of nightmare, eventually you're going to

13   wake up from. I was speechless, I didn't know how to

14   react. I didn't know what to do.

15   Q   You said your mom was there?

16   A   Yes, she was.

17   Q   Was anybody else there at the moment that

18   you first learned about this?

19   A   I don't remember seeing anyone else there.

20   I know that my brother was there somewhere, but he

21   wasn't, I don't remember him being in the room at the

22   time.

23   Q   How long did you stay at Bellevue?

24   A   I was there from the date of the accident

25   and I was discharged on May 17th.

26   Q   So from April 22nd, 23rd to May 17th?

2   A   Correct.

3   Q   And without getting through the

4   day-to-day, we don't want to take that much time.

5   And can you give the jury a general

6   idea of what was going on there, what you did over the

7   course of those three weeks?

8   A   Sure. When I was first there, like I

9   said, I had go through a couple surgeries, so I stayed

10 on the intensive care floor where they continually

11 monitored my activities and the healing of the leg.

12   First they had to have a tube inside

13 of my leg to continually drain it and clean it to make

14 sure there wasn't any infection. I eventually had to

15 have that tube taken out and that was pretty painful.

16   And from there it was just a waiting

17 process. They had to come in and check every day on

18 the healing. Check my temperature to see if, like I

19 said before, if there was any infection.

20   And eventually, when they found, you

21 know, there wasn't any established infection, that it

22 was starting to heal up a little bit, I was moved down

23 to the rehab floor.

24   Q   Before you moved down to the rehab floor,

25 during a time period before that, were you in any pain

26 on a regular basis at the hospital?

2   A   Yeah, I was in pretty bad pain.

3   Q   Describe that to the jury.

4   A   They had given me a morphine drip which I

5   had control of it, it was like a hand-held button that

6   you push. Didn't matter how many times I pushed it, it

7   would only release it mostly every 15 minutes at the

8   maximum.

9   But I was told by the nurses that I

10   was supposed to press the button any time I felt pain

11   because they registered how many times I pushed it, and

12   they were able to look at that and determine how much

13   pain I was in depending on how many times I pressed the

14   button.

15   Q   And were you able to get out of bed during

16   the initial parts of your stay?

17   A   Actually, I had to remain on my back

18   pretty much the whole time I was in the hospital, due

19   to my hip. I didn't have any surgery on it, it was

20   just they had popped it back in and that was all they

21   had done.

22   So I'd been instructed to remain on

23   my back. I couldn't roll over on my sides or roll on

24   my stomach or anything like that. I had to stay on my

25   back the entire I was there.

26   Q   What did you do about when you needed to

2   go to the rest room?

3   A   At first I had a catheter and so I didn't

4   have to do so anything at that time.

5   But then eventually when they removed

6   that, I had to make my way. There was a bathroom in

7   the room that I was in, so I had to, with help from the

8   nurses and from my mom, made my way into a wheelchair,

9   then I was able to make it to the bathroom.

10   Q   How long did you have the catheter?

11   A   I don't remember the exact time. I know

12   they did take it out while I was still up on the

13   intensive care floor.

14   Q   Did that cause you any discomfort, having

15   that process of the catheter?

16   A   Oh, yeah, specially when they took it out.

17   Q   Now, let's talk about your rehabilitation

18   in the hospital for a little bit.

19   Give the jury an understanding how

20   you went about losing your leg and how the folks at the

21   hospital working to try to get you so that you'd be in

22   a place where you can get discharged and have some type

23   of function.

24   A   After it was said that I was okay to, you

25   know, move around with my hip and they moved me down to

26   the rehab floor, the day-to-day activities where I

2   would do both rehabilitative in terms of physical

3   activity and I would also do other types of activities

4   like they'd bring us into an area where there was a

5   kitchen and they helped us learn how to move around in

6   the kitchen, keep our balance and do other household

7   chores that we're going to have to do when we were

8   released.

9   Also, using the bathroom, getting

10 from your wheelchair or crutches on to the toilet, be

11 able to get back off again safely.

12   Q   How was your mind set, how were you

13 feeling during this process now where you got moved to

14 the rehabilitation unit and, you know, you were

15 learning how to transition to real life?

16   A   At first I was happy, I mean, I was happy

17 to get off the intensive care floor, be able to get

18 around again, kind of be active a little bit, a little

19 more lax on the rehab floor.

20   Once I started doing the rehab and

21 having to go through all that, it was really

22 frustrating, because you go from being able to do the

23 simplest thing like walk up and down the stairs, and

24 use the bathroom and go to the bathroom and stuff like

25 that, to having to learn that all over again.

26   So, it was really frustrating when I

2   first got down there.

3   Q   How did they teach you to use the

4   bathroom?

5   A   Well, they had like an example, like a

6   fake toilet set up and it had like a seat over it like

7   a chair seat and in terms of using the wheelchair, they

8   taught us how to bring the wheelchair up next to it,

9   and you have to transition yourself using the handles

10   from the wheelchair and the handles on the toilet seat

11   that they had, and pull yourself up on to it while

12   using the balance from my leg, from my left leg.

13   Q   Is it fair to say for a period of time

14   when you'd go to the bathroom even for urination that

15   you would sit on the toilet?

16   A   Yes, I had to. I didn't have any balance

17   at that time.

18   Q   Okay. And for how long did you stay

19   through out that period of rehabilitation before being

20   discharged?

21   A   I'd say I was on rehab for maybe a week

22   and a half. About half the time I was there I was on

23   the rehab floor.

24   Q   And before being discharged, Dustin, did

25   you have any concerns about going back home by

26   yourself?

2   A   I knew my Mom was going to be there, so

3   that helped out a lot, but I didn't know what to

4   expect. You know, I had been home for three weeks, and

5   knew what I could do while I was on the rehab floor.

6   The larger kitchen -- but the way, my

7   apartment was set up, it was a wide open space, so I

8   was concerned and the bathroom was farther away from

9   where my bed was, I didn't have a bathroom in the same

10   room, have that luxury.

11   So, I was worried about how I was

12   going to get to the bathroom constantly. I didn't have

13   any of the things they had at the hospital at the time.

14   I didn't have a shower chair or a seat to go over the

15   toilet or any type of handles or anything like that.

16   So, I was concerned about how I was

17   going to function in my own apartment.

18   Q   What was your status as far as what you

19   could do or couldn't do when you were discharged from

20   the hospital?

21   A   Well, when I was first discharged I had

22   crutches, I was able to move around just with my

23   crutches, I didn't have a wheelchair or anything at the

24   time.

25   But my limb was still really weak, I

26   couldn't crouch for very long substances. And I

2   couldn't stand on it. And I'm still working on my

3   balance, something I'm still getting used to, so I

4   couldn't stand for very long periods of time, I'd

5   always have to sit down if I was waiting.

6   Like I remember when I was

7   discharged, my Mom had to go get the car and I had to

8   wait in the waiting room still, because I wasn't able

9   to stand outside and wait, and also, in terms of the

10   weather conditions, it was raining out or anything like

11   that, I always had to be careful because all I had was

12   my crutches, and if those slipped, I was pretty much

13   going down.

14   Q   Do you recall the day you were discharged

15   from the hospital?

16   A   Yes, I do.

17   Q   Tell us what you recall about that day.

18   A   They weren't sure what day it was going to

19   be, so I kind of found out that day that I was going to

20   be discharged and I was pretty happy, I was ready to

21   get out of there. Right to get back to normal life.

22   And I was discharged and we, my mom

23   had driven in that day, driven the car in, and she came

24   and picked me up and we just went, we went home.

25   Q   At that time did you have any type of

26   prosthesis, prosthetic device to use for your leg?

2   A   No, at that time the incision on the

3   bottom of my leg still wasn't -- excuse me, wasn't

4   completely healed, so I wasn't able to get any type of

5   prosthesis yet.

6   Q   And when you left the hospital, did you

7   have at that time the opportunity to see the status of

8   the leg that had been amputated?

9   A   Yes.

10   Q   What did it look like?

11   A   I had to constantly keep it wrapped. So

12 it was still, it was still kind of swollen, had a lot

13 of fluids still, and the bottom was pretty bad, pretty

14 bad scar, pretty bad scab still trying to heal.

15   Q   What was it like when you looked down and

16 you didn't see your leg, the rest of your leg or your

17 foot there?

18   A   I try my hardest not to look at it at the

19 time. But whenever I did, you know, it was just

20 unbelievable. I didn't, I didn't, I couldn't believe

21 it. I didn't know what to do.

22   Q   Did you continue with any type of medical

23 treatment after your discharge?

24   A   Yes, I did.

25   Q   Okay, tell us about that.

26   A   I had to constantly, like I said, it

 2 wasn't healed, so I had to, when I first was

 3 discharged, I had to frequently go back for checkups

 4 to, they wanted to check on the status of the healing,

 5 see how it was doing, make sure everything was moving

 6 along nicely.

 7   Q   How frequently did you have to go back to

 8 the hospital to the clinic there?

9   A   I don't remember exactly, maybe like every

10   other week I would say the appointments were at first,

11   and once it healed, then they were, they were less

12   frequent.

13   Q   And as far as rehabilitation, and learning

14   how to make use and get around, how did you work on

15   that?

16   A   They had given me exercises when I left,

17   the person I was working with gave me a sheet of

18   exercises to work on when I was home, stretching and

19   trying to strengthen my quads and my hip again.

20   The main concern was with my hip

21   because they wanted to make sure when I get my

22   prosthesis, I was able to walk the best that I could

23   without any weakness.

24   Q   And did there come a time when you first

25   started the process of getting a prosthesis?

26   A   Yes.

2   Q   Tell us about that.

3   A   I'd finally found out that after one of my

4   checkups that it was healed completely and I was able

5   to get a prosthetic. I had been, when I was in some of

6   the hospital checkups, the person had come, a couple of

7   prosthesis companies had come in and talked with me,

8   and you know, advertise themselves and based on those

9   suggestions, I picked one specific company to do my

10   prosthetic.

11   Q   And who was that?

12   A   The name is Ultrapedics is the company

13   name, it's run by Eric S.

14   Q   Why did you decide to go with Mr. S

15   and his company?

16   A   They were located near where I was at the

17   time, they were in Brooklyn. He had been doing it for

18   a long time, 30 years, and what I really liked about

19   it, they were, they did custom made legs. Assessed

20   your situation, took his measurements, and really took

21   into account your lifestyle and what the type of person

22   you are, and tried to find the best way he could to get

23   a leg that would fit the person that you were.

24   Q   What did you talk with Mr. Swelski about

25   in discussing your lifestyle and what type of leg you

26   wanted to fit into that lifestyle?

2   A   Well, I explained to him that I'd been

3   physically active, you know, I worked out and I played

4   basketball and whatever other sports I could at the

5   time.

6   So I was concerned that I wouldn't be

7   able to have a leg that I could do all those things

8   with, I could move around and, you know, make these

9   feel comfortable again and be able to walk.

10   Q   When did this process start where you

11   worked with Mr. S on developing some type of

12   prosthesis?

13   A   I don't remember the exact date. When I

14   came in and went to his office for the first time, he

15   took a lot of measurements, and did stuff like that, we

16   discussed with what different types of leg there are.

17   You know, his process and how he

18   makes the casting and how he develops the leg and stuff

19   like that.

20   Q   And throughout this time period, what was

21   happening with regards to your job at Bergdorf Goodman?

22   A   I was lucky, I had just started, but the

23   manager I had at the time was a really nice guy and he

24   was able to talk with our Human Resources Department

25   and he got them to be able to give me disability

26   payment while I was out.

2   Q   And how long did you stay out of work

3   before returning in any measure?

4   A   I was out from the date of the accident

5   until late June, I came back part time.

6   Q   So just about a little more than a month

7   after discharge you went back part time?

8   A   Correct.

9   Q   And at that time did you have a prosthetic

10   leg?

11   A   No. I did have one, it was a temporary

12   one when I first went back, but it wasn't very

13   comfortable, so I never wore it.

14   Q   So, what did you do instead?

15   A   I just had to go to work just with my

16   crutches and just have my leg. I wore pants like

17   snap-on pants at the time. I just had my legs out, I

18   didn't have anything to wear on it.

19   Q   And you would commute back and forth with

20   crutches?

21   A   Yes.

22   Q   Did you work full days?

23   A   No, at the time when I first went back, I

24   started doing rehab, I had to go back to Bellevue and

25   do rehab with physical rehab with a person and I used

26   my temporary leg to do the rehab, but I would take it

2   off as soon as I was done and after that I would

3   usually go off to work and work, whatever time I got

4   there, until the end of the day.

5   Q   Around that time period now in the end of

6   June, how frequently were you doing rehabilitation?

7   A   I was going two times a week, Tuesdays and

8   Thursdays for about an hour, hour and a half.

9   Q   And what would you do during a time at

10   rehab?

11   A   We did different things on different days.

12   Whether I first started doing it, a lot was stretching,

13   getting, you know, my movement back, my range of motion

14   back and then eventually we moved on to different

15   things such as movement and strengthening my legs and

16   different types of things to work on my balance and

17   help me out with high balance.

18   Q   And how did you come along, how were you

19   progressing?

20   A   At first it was really challenging, like

21   I'd say the temporary leg wasn't very comfortable.

22   It's nothing like I have, the one now.

23   So I really didn't want to wear it as

24   much as I could, so when we first started doing it it

25   was really challenging to be on it and he really wanted

26   me to be on the treadmill and trying to walk.

2   The pain I was in with that leg, I

3   couldn't do it. So at first it was really difficult

4   but then as time went by and I got more used to it and

5   I got back, eventually when I got the leg I have now I

6   was able to be more active and really push myself while

7   I was there.

4   Q.   What were your goals at the time of

5   starting rehabilitation as far as where you wanted to

6   get as a result of getting a prosthetic leg and

7   working at it?

8   A.   My main concern when I first started was

9   I wanted to be able to walk the best that I could. I

10 didn't want to have any type of significant limp or,

11 you know, any dipping down or anything like that. My

12 main concern was to try to strengthen my legs and hip

13 to try to get myself back to a point where I could

14 walk and appear normal.

15   Q.   And currently you've been talking about

16 what you have now. Can you tell the jury what you use

17 as far as a leg now?

18   A.   Yeah. The difference between the one I

19 have now and my temporary one, the temporary one was

20 just about as basic as you can get. You probably have

21 seen them before. It has a basic casting. Basic

22 mold. And then just a straight bar. And that's it,

23 with a base as the foot.

24   The difference between that and the one I

25 have now is, the one I have now has a pump on it where

26 the bar would be. And the way that the pump works is

2   every time I step, it pumps the air out of the socket

3   I have, and it's able to hold the prosthetic to my leg

4   tightly.

5   Q.   And how often during the day do you wear

6   your prosthesis?

7   A.   I wear it from the time I wake up until

8   sometimes I'll have bad days where I have to get home

9   and I will be in just too much pain, and I have to

10 take it off as soon as I get home. Most of the time I

11 wear it from the time I wake up until right before I

12 go down and go to sleep.

13   Q.   Does the device itself cause pain or

14 discomfort?

15   A.   It depends, because the way it works is

16 the sleeve that I have that goes over it, that holds

17 the leg to my actual leg, to the stump, is a major

18 component. And the problem with those sleeves is they

19 stretch out from wearing them and from me working out

20 and they break down. If there is any type of hole in

21 it at all, I'll lose that suction from the vacuum, and

22 it will be extremely uncomfortable and cause a lot of

23 pain.

24   Q.   What can you do now with your leg and

25 what can't you do? Give the jury an idea of how

26 you're able to adapt with it.

2   A.   I can -- Obviously I can walk again with

3   this leg. That's my main -- that's the main thing I

4   can do. I can work out. I can be on a treadmill. I

5   can walk, maybe jog for a couple minutes, not very

6   high speeds and for not very long. I can do just my

7   basic functions. I can go up and down stairs. I can

8   climb, do all of those things.

9   MR. SMILEY: With the Court's permission,

10   would Dustin be able to come down, I'll bring a

11   chair for him, so he could show the prosthesis to

12   the jury and the status of his leg?

13   THE COURT: Yes.

14   Q.   Dustin, at my request, so not to cause

15   anybody any awkwardness, did you wear some gym shorts

16   under the jeans that you have on now?

17   A.   Yes.

18   Q.   Okay. Would it be okay with you, what I

19   would like you to do is take off your pants so we

20   could show the jury your prosthesis, give them an idea

21   and explain it to them and show the current status of

22   your leg. I'll bring out a chair for you right here.

23   I want to make sure everybody can see.

24   MR. SMILEY: Is that okay for the jurors

25   in the back?

26   JURY PANEL: Yes.

2   Q.   Do you want to take off the sock down

3   there also. Okay. Now can, you know, as you're

4 seated here, can you explain for the jury what they're

5 looking at here that's on your right leg?

6   A.   I'll start at the bottom. This part

7 right here (pointing), you can see it's a little

8 broken, but it's a basic foot covering that they give.

9 You can see it's hollow on the inside, just looks like

10 a basic foot. This is something that comes with it so

11 that you can walk and it gives a flat movement.

12   MR. SMILEY: Let the record reflect or

13   may the record reflect, your Honor, that the foot

14   Dustin is referring to looks like a fake beige

15   bare foot, which is a covering that goes over the

16   prosthetic actual item.

17   THE COURT: Yes.

18   A.   And the type of foot I have, it's called

19 an action foot. As you can see, it's titanium plated.

20 And what it does is gives me the ability so when I

21 step down, this gives away a little bit. When I step,

22 your foot becomes a little bit more flat. So, it's

23 not like you're stepping down like that. It gives it

24 more leeway. So, when it comes down.

25   This part right here (indicating) is what

26 I was talking about with the pump. As you can see,

2 the tubing goes up into the bottom of the casting of

3 the leg. Every time I take a step, every time I put

4 pressure on the leg, the pump moves. I can't show you

5 as well. When I step, the pumps move in a little bit.

6 It pumps the air from, I believe, the side of this

7 cast out through the tube and out through the bottom.

8 So, I can maintain the suction on my leg.

9 This part right here (pointing), it's

10 made of micro fiber. This is the basic mold of the

11 leg, if that's how you want to call it. And then this

12 sleeve that you can see right here (pointing), this is

13 the basic sleeve that holds, you know, my actual leg

14 onto inside of this part of the leg.

15 If you can see, you know, you can see

16 that the pump is working. I don't know if you guys

17 can see it as well, but you can see the outline of --

18 outline of the leg inside the pump, that's kind of a

19 way for me to be able to judge if it's maintaining

20 suction. If I look at this and I don't see any type

21 of outline or anything like that, I know there must be

22 some type of hole in there or something where the air

23 isn't being held inside tightly.

24 Q.   And how would you go about taking this

25 off? In other words, on a typical evening, when would

26 you take off your -- your prosthetic device? Would it

2 be when you get home? When you sit on the couch? Or

3 before bed?

4   A.   Like I said, it depends on what type of

5   day I had. Where it's a day I had to walk and stand,

6   I had to stand on the bus or train on the way home, I

7   might be in a little bit of pain. I might take it off

8   as soon as I get home. Other than that, I usually

9   just wait until right before I get into bed. I'm

10   literally sitting on my bed and take it off and just

11   roll over.

12   Q.   Can you show the jury how you take it

13   off?

14   A.   Yeah. The basic sleeve slides right

15   down, slides off. You can see the inside of it. It's

16   molded. It's specifically molded. When I went to

17   Eric, he takes plaster and molds it around my leg and

18   makes this cast out of the plaster mold. That he

19   does.

20   My leg doesn't go all the way down to the

21   bottom. There is a section on the bottom space in

22   between, and that's what this pump is for, to pump

23   that air and keep it tight on my leg. That's the

24   basic setup of the leg.

25   MR. SMILEY: With the Court's permission,

26   may I bring this closer to the jury, the

2   prosthetic device?

3   THE COURT: Yes.

4   (Whereupon Mr. Smiley displayed the

5   prosthetic device to the jury.)

6   Q.   Now, Dustin, what do you -- what do you

7   currently have now covering the stump of your leg that

8   you still have?

9   A.   These right here are basic socks that I

10   got from the prosthetic guy (indicating). And the

11   purpose of these is when he takes the mold, the stump

12   itself, it increases in volume and loses volume. It

13   depends on a lot of different factors, the weather,

14   how much I'm on it, if I gained any weight, if I lose

15   any weight. It depends a lot.

16   So, this loses volume from the time he

17   has taken that cast. And the purpose of these socks,

18   I actually always have to carry a couple of these

19   around, additional ones around with me wherever I go,

20   because if at any point I feel any pressure in one

21   specific spot or any pain, then I'm suppose to take

22   the leg off and check and see if there is any redness,

23   any specific spot. And if so, I might have to take

24   some of these socks off or put some on to help my leg

25   fit in there better, to make sure it's not going down

26   too far.

2   Q.   Now, when you took off those two socks, I

3   see still left on your leg is some type of jell

4   device?

5   A.   Yeah. This is a jell liner. This is the

6   initial thing that goes on every morning. This goes

7   on. Obviously you don't have to wear these socks.

8   When he first designs the leg, it's intended not to

9   wear any of these. You wear like an initial kind of

10   pantyhose type stocking that comes up to about here

11   (indicating). I have to wear these. This goes on

12   initially, and this is the basis of the inside of it.

13   Q.   Would you mind removing the jell liner so

14   the jury can see your leg?

15   A.   Yeah.

16   Q.   And can you tell the jury what they are

17   looking at here?

18   A.   As I mentioned before, sometimes red

19   spots show up. You can see right here on my shin

20   there is a red spot right there (indicating), which

21   means I'm probably sinking down into that a little too

22   far. And so I probably have to add another layer

23   sometime today. And that's just stuff that I should

24   check constantly throughout the day. Check if I have

25   any spots anywhere specific. And if I do, like I

26   said, I have to add socks. The leg is breaking down a

2   little bit right here (indicating).

3   Q.   Indicating to the inside part of your

4   right knee?

5   A.   Right, the inside part. You can see

6   there is a little bit of a callous there. It's from

7   rubbing up against like this (indicating). One of the

8   legs -- one of the cases I had prior to this one was a

9   little too tight up here, and it would constantly push

10   on the inside of my leg and on the outside. So, I had

11   to have that one redone as you can see. But every

12   once in a while, depending on what type of shoes I'm

13   wearing or if I'm sinking down too far, it will rub up

14   against that and it will break down the skin.

15   Q.   Now, if you didn't have your prosthesis

16   on and you didn't have any assisted device, would you

17   be able to get around in this situation?

18   A.   Probably with by crawling. I wouldn't be

19   able to totally move around. I've been told not to --

20   I've been told by the doctors and by the rehab people

21   not to hop anywhere just due to the condition of my

22   hip and also, you know, if I got used to constantly

23   hopping around, they are afraid it could wear and

24   tear, wear and tear on my hip.

25   Q.   Okay. Now, can you just go through the

26   process, please, of putting your prosthesis back on?

2   A.   Sure.

3   Q.   As you would typically do in the morning

4   time.

5   A.   I need --

6   Q.   You need something?

7   A.   Yeah. I need a spray bottle. This is

8   just a spray bottle that I need. It's a combination

9   of water and a small amount of rubbing alcohol. The

10   purpose of this is this jell is kind of sticky. So, I

11   can't exactly just put it right on. I need to spray

12   the inside of it with this combination, so that when I

13   slide it on, it's a little bit easier to move right on

14   over the leg. So, I have to spray the inside of this

15   a little bit.

16   And then this one, this liner is designed

17   so there is actually a knee spot for my knee right

18   there (indicating). So, I have to line it up so that

19   that knee spot will cover over my knee. So, I have to

20   line it up with the end like that and just slide it

21   slowly on, all the way up. And sometimes, luckily

22   right there I don't have to, but sometimes in the

23   mornings I'll have to do this maybe two or three

24   times, because it's important to make sure there is no

25   space at the bottom of this. Sometimes I will do it

26   and it won't -- you know, I'll maybe miss a spot or,

2   you know, it might get stuck, and I might move it

3   down, and there will be air in the bottom.

4   It is really important that I have the

5 bottom part completely up against the bottom of the

6 stump to make sure that there is no air or discomfort.

7 So I can't really -- You know, this isn't moving

8 around on my leg. So, sometimes I'll have to do that

9 maybe two or three times to make sure it's good, but

10 luckily that time I got it on my first try.

11   And then I have to put the socks on over

12 the covering. Basic like you are putting it on your

13 foot almost. Slide it up. I try to lay this part

14 down a little bit (indicating). I have to make sure

15 that it doesn't come up over this (pointing), because

16 this is the part that suctions to this other part and

17 holds it tight. So, I have to make sure that the sock

18 doesn't come up to that part. This little space here

19 isn't suppose to be here, but I need a new one of

20 these.

21   Again with the socks, I also have to make

22 sure that they are snug on here and there is not any

23 wrinkles or any movements like that (indicating). I

24 couldn't put it on like that. But I really have to

25 pay attention to every detail of when I put this on,

26 because just the slightest thing, if I do it wrong, I

2 will notice right away, as soon as I put that on. It

3 will cause discomfort, and I will have to take it off

4   and do the whole process over again to make sure I'm

5   as comfortable as possible.

6   Q.   Dustin, on a day like today, when it's

7   really cold out, does it have any bearing on what you

8   need to do as far as the liners and the socks?

9   A.   Actually not when it's cold out, when

10   it's hot out. In my experience, it tends to be when

11   it's really hot, my leg kind of swells up a little

12   bit. During those days I, you know, I usually change

13   a lot of socks. Like in the beginning of the day I

14   will have like one sock on. By the end of the day,

15   because my leg has been in there so long, and it won't

16   be kind of swelled up from the heat, 'cause it's been

17   in there, I will have to take it off and put a couple

18   of more layers of socks on by the end of the day.

19   So, after I have all of this on, then I

20   have to fit it inside the leg. I usually have a shoe

21   on when I do this.

22   Q.   Do you need help?

23   A.   No. So, after I slide it in like that, I

24   make sure it's in like all the way. You know, I've

25   been told that it -- if you could see the circle, my

26   kneecap is right here (indicating). It should come

2   right below my kneecap. It shouldn't be too tight on

3   my kneecap or pushing it up, because that can cause

4   any type of damage or pressure on my knees.

5   After I have it on like that

6   (indicating), then I move this blue -- this is like a

7   blue cover on. It covers, 'cause this part of the

8   leg, these parts (pointing) can actually get kind of

9   sharp. After that, I pull this part up, over the

10   actual coverings of the legs, right here (indicating),

11   and then I just slide this slowly, slowly up like that

12   (indicating).

13   Again, it's important during this part

14   for me to make sure that I don't have any air pockets

15   back here and I didn't -- you know, nothing is stuck

16   behind my leg. It's smooth back there (indicating).

17   And I have to make sure that it's smooth all the way

18   up. And there is a space right here (indicating).

19   And it covers what I was showing you right here on the

20   jell liner (pointing), that it comes up over that.

21   And like I said before, it's smooth and it comes up a

22   good distance.

23   Q.   Relax. And then you have the foot

24   covering?

25   A.   Well, I don't usually take this off every

26   night. I don't have to take this off. So that's

2   usually on there already.

3   Q.   I see you're putting a sock over the

 4 prosthetic foot.

 5   A.   Right.

 6   Q.   Is that any type of special sock? What's

 7 the need for that?

 8   A.   Are you talking about this (indicating)?

 9   Q.   Yes.

10   A.   This sock just covers the basic foot.

11 And as you can see, there is a lot of -- You know, it

12 gets -- There is grease and oil down here. So, it's

13 basically to cover up the foot and just protect it

14 from any wear and tear that it might incur from being

15 inside this, this covering.

16   Q.   Now, I see on the covering you have it

17 looks like some type of grip tape or trainer's tape

18 around the foot. Can you explain that?

19   A.   Well, believe it or not, these things

20 right here actually are kind of expensive. And this

21 one broke on me right there (indicating), as you can

22 see from the foot, right there, coming through on the

23 bottom. So, instead of having to buy a new one, I

24 kind of tried to do a makeshift fix with some tape the

25 best I could.

26   Q.   Okay.

 2   A.   So, this just slides right back on. The

3   covering, like I said before, I usually don't take

4   that off. That usually remains on. And you can see

5   this tube. If you can see this tube right here

6   (indicating), that's a main part of the pump. I

7   usually have to check the tube to make sure there is

8   no cuts, any type of punctures like that.

9   So, I can, just after that, I can just

10   tuck that into the covering. And I usually wear some

11   type of -- I wear like a regular sock over the foot.

12   Sometimes I'll wear high socks. It depends, because I

13   really have to pay attention to this tubing, because

14   it's like the main part of the leg. I have to make

15   sure that no damaging happens to the tube. So,

16   sometimes I will wear a higher sock to make sure it

17   covers it, it doesn't catch on anything or caught up

18   and torn or anything like that.

19   Then in terms of putting my shoe back on,

20   I have these inserts that I have to, if I'm --

21   depending on what type of shoes I wear, I have these

22   black inserts. You can see this one is a little bit

23   thinner, but I have different thicknesses. Some are

24   really thick. Some are really thin like this

25   (indicating).

26   The purpose of these is the foot isn't

2   the exact length. So, I'm a little bit shorter on my

3   right side now. So, the purpose of these is depending

4   on what type of shoe I wear, whenever I have to get a

5   new pair of shoes, all the shoes I have now, I had to

6   test out and go through a lot of trial and error to

7   see what type of insert I needed with that. You know,

8   I would start with a thin one. I could tell right

9   away it's too low. I have to put a thicker one in.

10 Whenever I switch my shoe or use a different shoe, I

11 have to try to find the best insert to put in it.

12   Also sometimes with my shoes, I will have

13 a tendency to lean a little bit to my right. So, I

14 also have inserts that are just like this same thing

15 but cut in half. So, it will be a half of this. So,

16 I will put this along with the half of the insert

17 sometimes in some of my shoes so that when my foot

18 comes down, it's not coming down to the right. It's

19 coming down more on a balanced plain.

20   And I usually have -- I usually have a

21 shoehorn to help me get my shoe on. Like I said, I

22 have a shoehorn next to my bed, on my dresser, that I

23 use, 'cause sometimes the shoes, they are a little bit

24 difficult to get on over the foot. You know,

25 different shoes are harder to put on than others. So,

26 I just line up the shoe typically.

2   Usually I have a shoehorn for this part.

3   Then I just slide it on. And I always have to make

4   sure whatever shoe I'm wearing is as tight as I could

5   possibly tie it. Because I can't have it loose at

6   all. If my foot is coming out of the shoe at all or

7   anything like that, I will tell right away. And it

8   will really have an impact on how I'm able to walk.

9   So, I always have to make sure that I tie

10   the shoe possibly as tight as I can. I usually tie it

11   in a double knot. And that's the process.

12   Q.   Okay. If you want to put your other shoe

13   on, and then I ask you to take your time to get back

14   to the witness stand, and then we'll continue. I'll

15   give your wallet to your mom if that's okay.

16   A.   Yeah, that's fine.

17   Q.   Thank you, Dustin.

18   A.   You're welcome.

19   Q.   Now, Dustin, you told us about what you

20   can do with that foot and that leg, the artificial

21   foot and leg. Can you tell the jury about what you

22   can't do that you used to be able to do?

23   A.   Sure. As you can see, when you guys

24   looked at it, there is no ankle joint. So, the foot

25   basically has to stay flat. So, any type of jumping,

26   I have pretty much no ability really to any type of

2   jumping, any vertical at all.

3   Also as I mentioned before, running, I

4   can't run. I wouldn't even say jog. If I could jog

5   maybe on a treadmill, maybe like a couple minutes, but

6   I can't do any type of running, any sprinting,

7   anything like that. So, really makes it hard for me

8   to play any type of sports or, you know, even go for a

9   jog or a run in the morning, working out.

10   The other thing with the leg is with the

11   pump, I'm only allowed to have a certain amount of

12   weight on it. And I weigh, like I mentioned before,

13   about 190 pounds. And the maximum amount of weight

14   for the pump is 220. So, I have to really make sure

15   that whatever I have, I can't carry or have any

16   additional weight of more than 30 pounds on me, which

17   makes it hard for me to work out. I can't use any

18   type of free weights or anything like that. I always

19   have to use stationery machines.

20   And then also when me and my brother

21   moved into our recent apartment, I couldn't be much

22   help during the move, because I can't -- I couldn't

23   carry -- you know, I couldn't carry a couch up the

24   stairs. I can't carry, you know, big bags or anything

25   like that. A lot of the stuff I carried was just

26   stuff that I had to carry in just one hand, because we

2   had to go up the stairs.

3   The other thing is stairs. I have to

4   always hang on to a railing just because I have decent

5   balance, but sometimes my foot gets caught. I won't

6   lift it high enough or I won't bring it forward

7   enough, and it will get caught on the stairs.

8   Whenever I go upstairs, I always make sure I have a

9   grip on a handle somewhere. During the move I had to

10   make a lot of trips, because I could only carry a

11   certain amount of things, which made that really

12   difficult.

13   Q.   Physically as far as sports, things that

14   you used to do for fun and enjoyment before your

15   injury, what can't you do anymore that you used to

16   enjoy doing physically?

17   A.   I used to play a lot of basketball with

18   the people I worked with at the time at Bergdorf

19   Goodman. We used to go over to the New York Sports

20   Club that was up the street, and we would play a lot

21   of pick-up basketball. I can't compete in that. I

22   mean, will go by the court by our apartment and I'll

23   shoot around. But I can't -- The other day -- This

24   last summer I was there and a couple kids asked me to

25   play a pick-up game, but, I mean, I can't compete with

26   them, with those pick-up games. I can't even, you

2   know, really run. Like I said, I have no jumping

3   ability. So, I usually just go and shoot around. So,

4   I can't compete in any of those.

5   We also have a company softball team, the

6   company I work for now. And I was asked if I wanted

7   to play on the team this last year, and I had to say

8   no, I can't 'cause I can't -- I can't run around the

9   bases or be in the outfield and, you know, run after a

10   ball or anything like that.

11   Q.   Anything else physically as far as

12   physical activities that you want to do that you can't

13   do?

14   A.   The leg itself is not waterproof. I

15   can't take it in any water. I can't get it wet. So,

16   pretty much any type of swimming I can't do, because I

17   can't -- you know, I can't go jump in a pool, jump off

18   from a dock into a pond or any type of those

19   activities.

20   We have a family tradition where me and

21   my brothers and all of my male relatives, we go up to

22   the Adirondacks every summer and we get a cabin. We

23   go and jump off the rocks and the cliffs into the

24   water. Ever since this happened, every year I have to

25   sit around and watch all -- watch them all do that

26   while I can't participate in any of that.

2   Q.   Socially has this injury that you

3   suffered and the loss of your leg had an impact on you

4   as far as your social life, Dustin?

5   A.   Yeah, it has. Back when I was -- before

6   the accident happened I would pretty much, if I got

7   invited to go on a vacation or just an event, you

8   know, a friend say hey, come over and have a couple

9   people over to my house something, it's something I

10   would always try to do. But when my leg the way it is

11   and the process that I have to go through in terms of

12   taking it off, like if I'm sleeping over somewhere,

13   since it happened, I avoid all of those. I make up

14   excuses. I tell them that I can't go there because I

15   have something else planned or something like that.

16   And I just -- You know, I'm kind of ashamed to tell

17   them that I can't. That's the reason I don't want to

18   do any of those things.

19   So, I turned down opportunities for

20   vacations. You know, someone saying, let's go to

21   Miami. I'm going to be flying into Miami this

22   weekend. Do you want to see if you can go with me.

23   And I make up, like I said, I make up excuses. I say

24   oh, I got something planned for this weekend. I can't

25   go because someplace, especially a warm weather place,

26   I don't wear shorts anymore. I just -- I don't go out

2   in public with any shorts. I don't want to have to

3   deal with, you know, the looks that people give you

4   and just the way that I look with shorts on. So, I

5   don't wear those.

6   So, going to anything warm with a beach,

7   I can't be on the sand with this, because I can't have

8   any -- take the risk of getting sand inside the pumps

9   and ruining the holes or any of those. So, I avoid

10   going to any type of beach or any situation like that.

11   Q.   What about dating, are you currently

12   involved with anybody?

13   A.   No. I haven't dated anyone since the

14   accident happened. Kind of bothers me. I mean, you

15   go out and you meet someone. And I just wonder to

16   myself, you know, what point am I going to have to

17   tell them. Is it something, I meet someone. Hey, how

18   are you doing. I have a prosthetic leg. It's not a

19   great way to open up a conversation.

20   So, I go out there and, you know, I

21   always battle with when do I have to do this. Then I

22   avoid a lot of situations like that, because I don't

23   want to have to do that. I don't want to have to get

24   to the point where, you know, maybe we've been on a

25   couple dates, and they don't know, and I tell them

26   about the leg, and then I don't get anymore dates. So

2   then I wonder to myself is it because of my leg or did

3   I do something.

4   I mean, it's something I always have to

5   make a decision on. And it really pushes me to avoid

6   those types of things.

7   Q.   Can you give the jury just a few examples

8   of things that people with two healthy legs might take

9   for granted that you run into problems with or have

10   run into problems with as a result of not having all

11   of your right leg?

12   A.   One thing that I can definitely think of

13   is stairs. Just going up and down stairs. You know,

14   back in the day, the house I grew up in, we had a set

15   of stairs in our house. And I would run up and down

16   those stairs and swing down them. I would be up and

17   down them in five minutes or five seconds. But you

18   take that for granted, because now -- I took it for

19   granted, because now any time I have to take stairs,

20   it takes me a considerable amount of time to go up and

21   down those stairs, especially depending on the

22   situations. Like in this weather, it's a little bit

23   colder, slippery. And ice and rain and snow, I have

24   to take special precaution going down the stairs,

25   because I can't feel what I'm stepping on with my

26   right leg. So, if I'm stepping on some ice or, you

2   know, a crack or a bump or anything like that, I won't

3   be able to tell till it's too late.

4   Another thing is getting up, going to the

5   bathroom. You know, wake up in the middle of the

6   night, maybe had too much water before you went to

7   bed. And you wake up in the middle of the night and

8   you have to go to the bathroom. No problem. You hop

9   out of the bed. Run to the bathroom, go. And you're

10   back in your bed in a matter of minutes.

11   With me, I can't do that. I have to

12   either put on my leg or I have to find my crutches and

13   make my way to the bathroom. And while I'm there, I

14   have to hold myself up, make sure I have my balance,

15   go through the whole process and get back in bed. And

16   it doesn't sound like -- maybe it might not sound like

17   a big deal, but it's enough to deter me from getting

18   up, out of my bed. Sometimes I will just hold it and

19   hold it and put it off until the very last minute,

20   when I just -- you know, I have no other choice but to

21   do that.

5   Q   Dustin, currently do you suffer from any

6   physical pain or discomfort as result of your injuries

7   from the accident?

8   A   Yes.

9   Q   Could you tell the jury what that's about?

10   A   My hip is fully healed, but sometimes when

11   I workout or if, you know, I'm walking around, or

12   standing for too long, it starts to hurt a little bit

13   because the way the leg is, I was told as much as I can

14   to put pressure on both legs while I'm standing, but

15   you can only do that for so long.

16   So a lot of time when I have to like

17   wait for the bus or the train, excuse me, I have to

18   lean on my left leg, and I put a lot of pressure on

19   that. Sometimes it takes its toll on my hip.

20   But in terms of the stump, the best

21   way for me to describe it, is it's like a burning,

22   tingling sensation that is constantly, I just

23   constantly have, every waking moment of every day.

24   Best way I think that I've been

25   describing it, when your foot first falls asleep, when

26   it starts to wake back up and it kind of hurts a little

2   bit and it burns a little bit, that's just the way it

3   constantly feels all the time.

4   Q   By the way, Dustin, previously you

5   mentioned you would travel, a friend invited you to

6   Miami. Have you experienced any problems involving

7   your prosthesis, whether it is something to fly or

8   travel or go through security or airport or here in

9   this courthouse?

10   A   Yes, probably airport security is

11   extremely tight now. With this leg, it sets off the

12   metal detector any time. For flying, any time I go to

13   the airport, as soon as I walk through the metal

14   detectors I have to explain to them, you know, what the

15   deal is. Then they put me in one of those side rooms

16   where I have to pull up, you know, if I don't have any

17   type of pants that can be easily pulled up, I have to

18   take my pants off or down and they inspect the leg,

19   they wipe it down with something looking for like bomb

20   residue or anything like that. They wipe that down,

21   run their tests, and then maybe like 10, 15 minutes

22   process, at the least to wait and go through that.

23   So any time I'm going to fly

24   somewhere, I always have to give myself some extra time

25   because that happens every time, it's not, it's not

26   uncommon for me to do that, because they always make me

2   do that any time I go through the metal detector, but

3   any place that has metal detectors, sets it off

4   anywhere.

5   So any time I go through that, I

6   always have to explain to them, I have to show them the

7   components, show them the leg or anything like that,

8   any time I go through security.

9   Q   Dustin, as you sit here today, do you have

10   any concerns about your future and about the fact of

11   your injury or your ability to do or not do things that

12   you had planned for the future?

13   A   Yeah. You know, it changed my whole

14   outlook on my future. I'm big, we have a big family, a

15   our family is really important too, that's the way I

16   was raised, and I have on my mind a lot of things we

17   did when we were young, when we were family, it's

18   something I always wanted to be able to do with my

19   kids.

20   You know, for example, back at our

21   house we used have to a pond in the back of our house

22   and we would go down there and we'd be down there and

23   one of the big things was we used to race my dad out in

24   the pond and we used to try to catch him, and I know

25   that, I know that I'm not going to be able to do that

26   if I have any kids or anything like that.

2   I'm not going to be able to have any

3   races with them or help them out with basketball or

4   football or participate with them in any sports or

5   anything like that.

6   Also I'd like to own a house

7 eventually, and I just don't know if I know what it

8 takes to -- from my dad and my mom had go through to

9 upkeep a house, and I just don't know if I'll be able

10 to, whether I'm, you know, I might be able to do it

11 now, but what about when I'm 55, 56 years older, I'm

12 not going to be able to climb on ladders, clean up the

13 gutters on the house, or do any repairs or paint a

14 house.

15   That stuff is a real concern to me,

16 because it's all things I wanted to be able to do when

17 I get older, it wasn't something I thought was ever

18 going to be a problem for me.

19   Q   What impact, as best you can describe it,

20 has the injuries that you suffered caused on you

21 emotionally, the type of person you are?

22   A   What I've been told by people before the

23 injury I was very outgoing, I participated a lot in

24 conversations and I was very outgoing with people,

25 meeting new people. I never had a problem with that.

26 Or I was always very, I won't say cocky, I was always

2 very sure of myself, I had confidence in myself as a

3 person, and what my abilities were and now I know, I

4 just, I don't, best way for me to describe it, I just

5 don't have any confidence in myself, I don't feel like

6 I know what my capabilities are, and I don't feel like

7   best way I guess for me say, I don't feel like I could

8   do anything.

9   Back before the accident I felt I

10   could do anything I wanted to do. I could just be

11   anything I wanted to be. But I just don't feel the

12   same way now.

13   Q   Is there any particular part about the

14   injuries that you suffered that is worse than anything

15   else?

16   A   When I think of two things I'd like to

17   say, it's one part, but it's multiple parts, I mean

18   something like this. Not just one worse thing. Worse

19   thing for me, one of the worst things is the

20   uncertainty, like I said, I can move around now and I

21   can trip on something or maybe trip going up the stairs

22   and catch myself, but, you know, I don't know what I'm

23   going to be able to do when I'm an older, older man.

24   I won't have the capabilities I have

25   now. I don't know if I'll be able to handle myself and

26   take care of myself when I'm older. Like I don't know

2   what I'm going to be able to do. And that uncertainty

3   of my future, not knowing, not knowing where I'm going

4   to be, where I can go, what I'm able to do, it really,

5   really bothers me and eats at me.

6   And then the other thing that gets to

7   me is the pain that I'm in every day, but also, the

 8   pain that I know I've caused my family and the people

 9   that have had to go through, people have had to go

10   through this with me.

11   And I know my mom especially --

12   excuse me. I know my mom especially, she's spent time

13   with me since the accident happened, on her, so I know

14   I put them through this kind of pain and suffering as

15   much as I have to go through. It's really been hard on

16   me.

17   Q   Thank you, Dustin.

18   MR. SMILEY: I don't have any further

19   questions.

CHAPTER 4

CROSS-EXAMINATION

This chapter explains how to conduct a cross-examination of a lay or expert witness in a personal injury case. It will provide the tools you need to effectively cross-examine a witness, even if you've never done it before. You will learn the appropriate way to prepare a cross-examination through digesting transcripts, creating an outline, and laying the foundation for impeachment. Even if you have experience with cross-examining witnesses, you might learn something new from this chapter. Or you might feel reaffirmed that you're already doing it the right way. At the very least, you'll be able to go toe-to-toe with your spouse, child, or parent. My mother always likes to say, "Don't cross-examine me, Andrew."

There are several key areas covered in this chapter:

Preparation. "Preparation, preparation, preparation" is my mantra. It's so important to prepare for every aspect of a trial, but it's especially crucial in cross-examination. If you've ever observed a good cross-examination, it's not that the lawyer is so brilliant that they're coming up with everything off the cuff. Behind the scenes, a lot of preparation went into it, allowing them to look smooth, sharp, quick-witted, and prepared.

Creating a plan. You always need to have a plan, whether it's in direct-examination or in cross-examination. What do you want from this witness? You need to know how to digest a transcript. That means going through a pre-trial deposition transcript, highlighting the important stuff, making sure that information is accessible, and using it to prepare and conduct a cross-examination.

Researching the witness. Not everybody takes this step, but it can be very effective and make a difference in your case.

Identifying the points you want to make when you cross-examine. You don't just get up in a trial and ask questions. You must have a purpose to your line of questions, whether it's establishing (or eliminating) a *prima facie* element in the case, attacking a witness's credibility, or getting important items into evidence. Those are the "apples" you want to acquire for your summation basket.

How to prepare the outline. You need to have an outline for cross-examining. You won't read it during cross-examination, but it will help you stay organized and serve as a safety net if you lose your train of thought.

Courtroom position. Courtroom position is important when you are cross-examining a witness, and it's not always the same as in direct-examination.

How to control a witness. Not all witnesses sit there and give you nice answers. Sometimes, especially when they're expert witnesses, they're long-winded, they don't answer you, or they challenge your questions. If they don't respond appropriately, you can impeach them in cross-examination. One of the most powerful moments in the courtroom is when you pull out something from their prior testimony that contradicts what they've just said to the jury.

How to wrap up your cross-examination. As with every other aspect of the trial, you want to finish strong.

Preparing and Planning for Two Types of Witnesses

There are two types of witnesses, lay witnesses and expert witnesses. A lay witness is someone who's not getting paid to testify. It could be the driver in a car accident case, a friend of the defendant or the plaintiff, a family member, a non-party witness, or someone else who has information relevant to the case to share.

An expert witness is paid to testify as an expert in a particular area. That could be a treating physician in a medical malpractice case, a liability medical expert, an engineer, an economist, or another type of expert. Expert witnesses are usually more challenging to question than lay witnesses, because of their "expertise" in the subject upon which they are testifying. But with the right preparation, it's not a problem.

69

In your preparation, think about what type of witness you have and ask yourself what you want to get from this witness. What do you want to talk about in your summation that you need to pull out of this witness's testimony? Is this a witness who's going to hurt your case? Do you need to discredit them or show that whatever they're attempting to say is a bunch of nonsense, and highlight that to the jury so they can't hurt the case? Could this witness help your case, even if it's a witness for your adversary? Maybe there are helpful things that you can draw out from that witness on cross-examination.

Most of the time, it's a mix of both. You usually can draw out things that can help your case and cut down on whatever they may have said on direct to hurt your case. Again, you want to get these "apples" into your summation basket. So, you need to have a plan for what you want from your witness.

Digesting Your Transcripts

I don't try criminal cases, but my understanding is that you don't have pre-trial depositions in criminal litigation. You don't have the benefit of prior sworn testimony to use to prepare. So, all questioning of a witness is truly "off the cuff." In civil cases, you generally will have pre-trial deposition testimony and transcripts you can use. You'll certainly have it for all the main witnesses. Experts usually are not deposed in civil cases except in Federal Court. You want to gather every transcript available containing prior sworn testimony for the witness you will be cross-examining.

With an expert witness, you can often obtain transcripts from other cases. Lawyers are usually pretty open about sharing transcripts, especially if you're on the same side of the case. So, if another plaintiff's lawyer reaches out to me and says, "The defense is calling William Head again, the doctor who has been doing independent medical examinations for 40 years. Do you have any transcripts?" I'll say, "Sure, I'll give you all my transcripts."

If you reach out, do your homework, and call the lawyers affiliated with cases who may have cross-examined that expert, they're usually happy to share transcripts. You can get good tidbits to use in your cross-examination, especially if they're testifying on the same specific subject matter as in your case.

Once you get the transcripts, you can start to digest them. I like to use a yellow legal pad to digest my transcripts. Some people like to type. I sit on my couch with my yellow pad, some red pens, and the transcript. It's pretty mindless work. You can do it while the TV is on and you're watching a football game, but it's crucial to get it done. I go through the transcript and write a page and line number in the left column, and a statement from the transcript on the right:

Deposition of Defendant
    John Smith - Train Operator
        11/20/14

page	
2:5	Employed as train operator for 5 years
3:10	Trained to look for people on tracks
2:18	Aware people can fall on tracks or for
-25	other reasons be on tracks
12:9	Entered the station travelling 30 mph
14:11	Saw plaintiff on tracks but thought garbage
14:15	middle of platform
15:2	I was 3 car lengths away
15:10	I honked horn then put brakes in emergency
20:12	Was 1 car length away when put brakes in emergency

Transcript example. The above example is from the deposition of a train operator in a subway accident case from November 20, 2014. On the left side, under "page," I have 2:5, which means it's page two, line five of the transcript. Below that, I have 3:10, page three, line 10, and 3:18-25, page three, lines 18 through 25. Sometimes I'll paraphrase or summarize. The 3:18-25 was testimony where this train operator responded that he was aware that people could fall on the tracks for various reasons.

71

I'll go through the transcript, and if there's a really good statement that I know I want to highlight, I underline it in red. For example, someone might say, "I don't know what color the traffic light was." If it's a quote, sometimes I'll put quotes around it. In the preceding example, I've underlined that this train operator saw my client on the tracks and thought he was garbage, not a person. I've underlined that he was three car lengths away when he first saw what he thought was garbage on the tracks, which was actually my client, passed out. And I've underlined that he was one car length away when he put on the emergency brakes.

Whether it's the train operator, the driver of a car, or an expert witness, I do this "digesting" through the entire transcript. This one page is an example, but I'll go through a 300-page transcript and multiple legal pages of digesting.

It's crucial to have this digest. It is the foundation of preparing and building your cross-examination. It's an index that tells you where all the good stuff is and how to get to it quickly. And in the process of going through the transcript, underlining, circling, or starring things, whatever works for you, you'll be able to start picturing what you have on the page.

During your cross-examination, you'll remember seeing "three car lengths away" underlined in your digest. You'll bring the digest with you in case you need to look at it during the trial. You'll see, "Oh, this was at 15:2." You'll know where everything is, which will be important for impeachment (discussed a bit further on in this chapter). So, you should digest every transcript you have for a lay witness or an expert witness before preparing your outline.

Researching Your Witnesses

The next thing you should do is research the witness you will be questioning. You want to get all the information down first, before you start working on your outline and your points. You want to see what information you have on this witness. So, after I digest the transcripts, I like to research the witness.

Today, the things we can find out about people online are amazing. I always Google a witness before conducting a deposition and before cross-examining them. You can also look up the Jury Verdict Reporter, which is a nationwide database where you can look up expert witnesses.

You can look in Lexis, Westlaw, PACER, e-Law, eCourts, or other online legal services for information about witnesses.

I often find great stuff on Instagram and Facebook. In a ski accident case, I had two patrollers giving different versions of the post-accident investigation. I was about to question one of them, so the night before, I Googled her. Sure enough, I see her Instagram, which is public. And I see a guy next to her. She has her arm around him, and she's kissing him, and it's the other patroller. I thought, "Ah, they're a couple. How did they not discuss this?" You never know what you can find, so it's really important to look.

In Dustin's subway accident case, the defense for the New York City Transit Authority called in a toxicologist from Florida, and I figured he was a pretty prominent expert—why else would they fly him to New York for this case? I looked up his curriculum vitae and saw a lot of credentials. The night before I was going to cross-examine him during the trial, I started doing some online research. Sure enough, I came across a stipulation of settlement signed by this witness online. I was able to print it out with his signature. It was an agreement with the Attorney General's office, saying, "I hereby agree that I will not practice toxicology in the state of New York for six years." This was a result of some wrongdoing going on at a toxicology lab he ran in New York. And now I knew why this witness was in Florida, being flown in. It must have been something the defense overlooked, or this witness didn't share with them.

I brought the stipulation he signed to trial the next day, and let it loose on cross-examination. The defense wasn't happy. The jurors' jaws dropped. I said, "Oh, that's why you came in from Florida, because you're not licensed to practice in New York. You got kicked out of New York, didn't you? You agreed not to practice in this state because of wrongdoing at your lab, correct?" You can often find interesting stuff, so it's really important to take a moment and do some research.

Identifying Your Points

Once you've gathered as much information as possible on the witness by digesting transcripts of prior testimony and doing research online, it's time to start thinking about the points you want to make, the sections you are going to touch on, and the areas that are important. You

73

want to get the apples in your basket for your evidence. You should create five to ten sections in your outline covering what you want to go over and the information you want to elicit.

Collateral issues. Collateral issues should be a section of your digest. Collateral is the fact that this toxicologist was kicked out of New York. Collateral is the fact that Dr. Head has probably examined over a thousand people and made millions of dollars; not one of them has ever been on behalf of a plaintiff. You want to have a section on prior criminal convictions, prior lawsuits or accidents, or any other collateral issues.

Sometimes you don't need to go there. But if you think a witness is going to attempt to hurt you—usually that's an expert called by the other side whose sole goal is to rebut your case—you want to be able to highlight the fact that the jury is not hearing an objective opinion. You can't say it explicitly, but what you want to highlight to the jury through your questioning is that, "This is a hired gun."

In Oscar's motorcycle accident case, we had an excellent accident investigation engineer who had all kinds of re-creations, measurements, drone footage, and maps we were able to use to reconstruct the accident. In rebuttal, my adversary brought in an engineer who I knew to be frequently retained by defense firms. At the end of this chapter, you can find my cross-examination of this defense expert. I encourage you to take a moment and read through it—I think you'll enjoy it.

I was trying to highlight that in his direct, he was trying to come across as a scientist who could reconstruct how the accident happened, but in reality, he didn't base any of his opinions on science. He didn't measure anything. He didn't include any diagrams. I went out of my way to undercut him and say things like, "You're not… you haven't based this on… this isn't objective." And then I segued into saying, "And you're not really here objectively. You're here for the defense counsel's law firm, right? Don't you do a lot of work for his firm?" My adversary objected but got overruled. These questions of an expert witness are not only fair game, but important and impactful to a jury.

During my cross-examination of the defense expert witness, I brought out that he previously testified 15 times at trial for this defense firm and reviewed over 100 cases for them. I asked how much he charges for the reviews and for trial testimony. And then I said, "So it's fair to say you've made over $100,000 just from this law firm alone, right? And you want this jury to believe that your opinion, without any measurements or diagrams, or any of the other information that our expert provided for them, is really objective?"

You want to decide when you will use the information in your outline. I try to save the collateral stuff for right after the witness has given me a hard time, not given me a straight answer, or thinks they made a point. You want to hit them at the right time.

Preparing Your Outline

Here is a portion of the cross-examination outline I prepared for the subway train operator based on the digest example I shared on the preceding pages:

Cross of John Smith

I. EXPERIENCED OPERATOR - knew people on track

- 5 years train operator   2:5
- trained to look for people on track   3:10
- You knew and, in fact, were trained
  to be on lookout for people on tracks 3:18-25

II. Going Fast

- entered station going 30 mph   12:9
- didn't know speed limit
- slower you travel the faster you can stop

III. Didn't stop when he first saw ∏

- You saw something
- You were 3 car lengths away 15:2
- The cars on your train were 60 ft cars
- 180 feet away
- Didn't put brakes in emergency first
- First you honked horn 15:10
- Didn't put brakes into emergency until
  1 car length away from ∏ 20:12
- only 60 ft away!!
- Going 30 mph o!
- By then too late
- Your train struck and killed the plaintiff

In this outline, you will see I have three points I felt were important to make. The first point is to highlight that this is an *experienced operator*. I use that to my benefit. People are going to end up on the subway tracks. This is New York City, and you're trained to look out because people are drunk, do drugs, have heart attacks, pass out, slip, fall, and get pushed. People fall on the tracks, and it doesn't matter *how* they got there, you have to be on the lookout for them and be prepared to stop the train.

In my outline, I have numbers on the side—in red—taken from my digest. So, when I say, "Five years as a train operator," 2:5 (page 2, line 5 of the transcript) is where I'll find it. And then my question will be, "And sir, you are actually trained to look for people on the track. Isn't that correct?" And if the answer is different, I can impeach the witness because I know the answer to that question, in that form, is on page 3, line 10 (3:10).

Then in my second point, I wanted to highlight that he was operating the train too fast. "You're going fast. You entered at 30 miles an hour, and you didn't know the speed limit?" I wanted to highlight that more speed equals less time to stop.

Finally, in point three, I wanted to highlight that he didn't brake when he first saw something on the tracks, and if he did brake, the train would have stopped before running him over. "And you didn't stop when you first saw something on the tracks." So here, again, I'll say, "And you saw something, didn't you? And you were three car lengths away when you first saw something, weren't you? And a car length is 60 feet, so that's 180 feet away. You saw something with 180 feet of distance and time to stop the train."

If the witness says, "Well, I think I was closer. I was only 100 feet away" (in an attempt to claim it was too late to stop the train), I have the page and line number to impeach. You don't always have a page and line for everything you want to ask, but when it falls in that section, you want to walk them down the road to where you know you can nail them with what they've previously testified to.

You can always move your outline points around. As long as you know what each of your point sections are, then when you're actually doing the cross-examining, in your mind, you know the points you want to hit. I knew I was in my first section, "experienced operator." And I was thinking about what I wrote at the top of this page and these three points. Then I knew I had the section on, "You didn't stop when you first saw something on the tracks."

Preparing helps solidify information in your mind. For a lot of trial work, the process of writing things out, whether it's an outline or digesting, is a way to train your mind. Your mind absorbs this material through this process, so you don't have to keep looking at your outline when you're at trial. But if you need to, during your cross-examination, when you're ready to move on to a new point, you can take a break, walk over to the counsel table, have a sip of water, and look down at your outline.

In cross-examination, you have the digest and the outline next to each other. You're taking a lot of the points that you already have, from a transcript or otherwise, that you know you can get out of the witness. And then you're flipping them into questions.

For example, my question in the deposition at 15:2 was, "How many car lengths away were you when you saw something on the track?" And the answer was, "I was three car lengths away." At trial, I'm going to say, "You were three car lengths away when you saw something, correct?" And that gets into controlling the witness with leading questions. You take answers and information you know and flip it into an assertion they have to agree with. If they don't, you're going to impeach them. You know the answer.

Many lawyers say, "You never want to ask a question in cross-examination that you don't know the answer to." I would agree with that, but I would add, "Unless the answer doesn't really matter—if you're asking a question for the effect of it." But the idea with cross-examination is that you're controlling the witness by asking questions you know the answer to, or where you don't care what the answer is because you want to make a point. And you're ready to impeach them if they don't drop in line with where you're going. That's how you're going to set up your outline.

Now you have your outline, your sections, what you want for your summation basket, the points you want to make, what to bring out that'll help you, what to undercut that'll hurt you, and what collateral stuff you've got in your back pocket to bring in at the right time as a zinger to show the jury how you can discredit this witness. You have everything at the ready.

Recognizing That You're Not in Control

Cross-examination is a bit nerve-wracking, because it is the first time at trial when you don't have total control. You can try to have as much control as possible. But as a plaintiff, the way that a trial works for me is I give my opening statement, which I have total control of. The defendant gives their opening statement. And then, I call my first witness for direct exam, which I'm prepared for, as covered in Chapter 3. It's all seamless, choreographed, and smooth. We know what's going to happen.

But when you start cross-examining a witness, you don't know what will happen. Usually, the defense lawyer is first, because they cross-examine whomever I'm calling in my case-in-chief. And it's a little nerve-wracking because you're not sure how your witness will respond.

You don't need to beat up on a witness, raise your voice, or be aggressive to be a good cross-examiner. I tried a case against a formidable adversary many years ago. He was soft-spoken and stood at the podium and asked questions in a measured manner to elicit the answers that he wanted from my witness. It was very persuasive and compelling. So, you don't need to use your hands, raise your voice, or be aggressive just because it's cross-examination.

Some witnesses will just follow what you're saying and give it up. The conversation will be: "And you did this, right?"

"Yes, sir."

"And you did that, right?"

"Yes, sir."

"And you didn't—you didn't look where you were going."

"That's right, Mr. Smiley."

"You're completely at fault in this case, aren't you?"

"Yeah."

They just "Yes" you. You don't often get those, but sometimes it happens. So, when you're preparing your witnesses for direct and cross-examination, tell them not just to agree because the lawyer is saying something, but to *listen* to the question before answering. Because we lawyers try to get into that mode, where during cross-examination we can get the witness to sit and nod and say, "Yes, that's correct." "Yes, that's incorrect." That will happen more often with lay witnesses.

Expert witnesses may challenge you. Expert witnesses will fight you to the point where they won't even give you a straight answer. And a lot of professional experts, like the defense expert in Oscar's case, use different tricks so that they don't really have to answer your question. One trick this expert tried to use is, "Well, I can't answer that yes or no. I have to qualify. That's

79

a big thing. I need to qualify my answer. May I qualify?" And I always say, "No, you can't qualify. You can answer my question. And I'll ask it again. If you don't understand it, I'll rephrase it, but you have to answer my questions."

I was in a deposition where the witness was cagey, and she wouldn't answer my questions. She'd give long-winded answers. And I'd say, "That wasn't my question. Here's what I'm asking." And then the defense lawyers started saying, "Objection, asked and answered. The witness answered, you may not like their answer, but that's the answer." I didn't back off. I said, "No, they didn't answer my question. We'll read it back. And I'm going to keep asking it until I get the answer." That's what you have to do in your cross-examination. You don't stop until you get the answer you're looking for. Otherwise, you're bailing on your plan.

Positioning Yourself in the Courtroom

In terms of courtroom position, I don't like to stay at the back of the jury box, like I do in direct-examination. In direct-examination, as the lawyer, you want to blend in. You want your witness to be the star.

In cross-examination, you want the focus to be on the questions you're asking and on you and your incredulity. Let the jury see your disbelief in how you're asking questions or reacting. You can do that by not being stuck at a podium but by moving freely within the courtroom in the well. I get right up in their face, in that discomfort zone, when I ask questions. I like to move forward and back. I like to move a little closer, back up slightly, and move side to side. Some judges will not allow you to do that, but most do, so ask. You always want to ask the judge what the rules are about being behind the podium or whether you can move around.

During my cross-examinations, I usually talk with my hands moving. I'll be sarcastic. I'll look at the jury. You'll get a sense of that when you read the transcript at the end of this chapter.

I said, "You didn't measure that, did you?"

And he said, "Well, I approximated it."

I said, "Well, approximating isn't science. You just told the jury it was 100 feet, but where's your measurement?"

"Well, I did measure them."

"Where's the picture of your ruler? Where's the notation that you took down?"

"Well, it was approximately 100 feet."

"Approximate isn't science. We're here talking about science, right?"

And I'll look at the jury.

You can do that. If it's not your comfort level, you don't have to. But if you feel comfortable with it, you want to change your tone and your inflection. You can raise your voice slightly and say, "Come on!" When a witness fights you, for example, this witness kept saying, "Can I qualify? Can I qualify?" you can say, "No sir, you can't qualify. I'd really appreciate you answering the question so the jury can understand." You can throw out things like that. Let the jury see you're an advocate for them trying to get to the truth. You're not just doing your job. You're there to grill this witness for the benefit of the jury.

Sometimes, if you know what's coming, in your opening, you can say something like, "Members of the jury, I just want to give you a heads up. When I question their expert, I want you to pay a little extra attention when I get to the part about measurements. And let's see what we find out about that." You can cue them up a bit in your opening, which is a lot of fun.

You're going to want to look at the jury to get a little feedback. If you feel you're scoring some points, you can look over to the jury box and see if any jurors look like they agree with you. Sometimes they'll be rolling their eyes, and you get some good feedback that way. You don't know if it's true—I've had people smile at me who don't go my way—but cross-examination is the time to get some feedback.

Controlling the Witness

I recommend that you have your outline and your digest on the counsel table or the podium, next to each other. Then you ask the witness your leading questions. Chapter 3 covered open questions and non-leading questions in direct-exam. A leading question suggests the answer, and you're not allowed to suggest an answer to your own witness. But on cross-examination, that's

81

exactly what you want to do. You never want to open up the floor. You never want to say, "Can you tell us what you did in your evaluation of my client?" That expert will turn to the jury and take control for 20 minutes, saying something like, "Well, I'm very thorough. And I like to first review all the records, and I like to do this…."

You never want to hand the mic to them. You want to be in control. You never want to open it up, so a witness who's adverse to you can explain anything. And when they try to say, "Well, I want to explain," you say, "No, you answered my question." That's what direct/redirect is for. Later, their lawyer can say, "Mr. Smiley didn't want you to explain. But why don't you go ahead and explain now?" Nine times out of 10, that redirect isn't done. So, you cut them off. You're in charge. You ask leading questions such as, "Isn't it true that…" "Wouldn't you agree that…" Or, you make a statement and end it with "correct?" For example, "You were three car lengths away, correct?" Closed, leading questions are how you keep control.

If the witness isn't answering you straight or gives a long-winded answer, you can't cut them off. It gets frustrating. The witness rambles on and on without answering your question. The judge is getting frustrated, you're getting frustrated, and you feel like you can't get your answer. In that situation, you give it a couple of shots. If a long, lengthy response doesn't answer your question, you can say, "I appreciate that answer, but it wasn't an answer to my question. I'm asking you to please answer my question, which is as follows. Isn't it true that…" If they go on and on again, you can say, "I understand your hesitancy to answer my question, but you need to answer it, please. Can you do it in a yes or no?"

You may get some objections from your adversary. But it's fair game to ask a witness, "Can you answer this as a yes or no, please?" In my example, you'll see in my transcript that the judge got involved. Usually, the judge will get annoyed when a witness is not answering questions and is being cagey. They'll say, "Can you answer the question as a yes or no, please?"

You could always say, "Your Honor, the witness clearly is not answering my question. I'd ask the witness to be instructed to please give a yes or no answer if they can." You can do it that way also. But you never want to lose control. The way you regain control is with good, tight questions. Let the witness realize that when you're questioning, you won't tolerate them rambling on or asking to qualify answers.

82

Knowing How to Impeach

You don't argue with the witness. But you make it clear that if they don't answer appropriately, you're going to impeach them. That's the ultimate smackdown, and it's a lot of fun. If you set it up right and you're prepared, it can be very effective. And the digesting and the outlines are all set up for an impeachment.

To impeach a witness, first, you need to lock them into an answer. In my case, I wanted the train operator to agree that he was three car lengths away when he first saw something on the tracks. I might say to the witness, "You were three car lengths away when you saw something on the tracks, isn't that right?" If the witness says, "No, that's not right, sir." I'll say, "You're saying you were not three car lengths away?"

I'm not going to say, "How far?" yet. I'm going to lock them in, because I want to highlight the difference between what they're saying now and the prior testimony they gave (which I have digested). So the witness might say, "Well, I'm not so sure. It could have been one or two car lengths away." And I'll say, "So you're saying you're not sure? It could have been one or two car lengths away? Is that your testimony today?" You lock them down. They say, "Yes, that's my testimony. It could have been one or two car lengths away."

Now, I know that this witness testified under oath a year before trial that he was three car lengths away. That's important, because the further away you are, the more time you have to brake the train before it hits somebody. The further away the train is, the stronger my case is. So then I locked the witness down with the inconsistent answer at trial. The jury hears it. It's locked in. I'm making it very clear to the jury. I said, "That's your testimony today?" He said, "Yes, it is." I said, "Your testimony, you are maybe one or two car lengths?" He said, "That's right." Then you get into impeachment.

When you're impeaching a witness, you don't have to use specific, exact language, but the gist of the language has to be there. First, you need to establish through the witness that the witness testified previously in a pre-trial deposition. After you lock them down, you take a deep breath. They've given their answer. You look at your digest, which notes that their answer is on page three, line five. You open the transcript to page three, line five, and hold it up.

83

You say, "You testified at a deposition in this case previously, right? Last year, June 20th, right? Do you recall that?" The witness says, "Yes, I do." If the witness says no to this question, you stand up and say, "I'd ask defense counsel to stipulate that the witness did testify on June 20th at a deposition." And then your adversary has to acknowledge it. If they don't, you show it to the judge.

So you start by locking them into acknowledging they took that deposition. Then you say, "And you were asked questions, like you're being asked questions in this courtroom today. And you gave answers, right?" Sometimes you're the person who did that deposition. You can say, "You remember? I asked you questions, and you gave answers." And they say, "Yes." Then you say, "And your answers were truthful, right? You took an oath to tell the truth at the start of that deposition, the same oath you took today, isn't that true?"

"Yes."

"And you did tell the truth."

"Yes."

"Under oath."

"Yes, I did."

"And there was an attorney there representing you, right? You were there along with lawyers sitting next to you?"

"Yes."

"And after the deposition, you had a chance to review that transcript and make any changes, right?"

"Yes." (When you're doing your digesting, you want to check that they didn't make any changes, and if they did, it wasn't for this question.)

Then you say, "And you didn't make any changes, did you?"

"No, I didn't."

"Do you recall being asked the following questions and giving the following answers at that deposition?"

And then, you have to identify the questions for the court, the court reporter, and your adversary. You can say, "Your Honor, counsel, I'm now referring to the witness's deposition transcript from June 20th of last year, page three, line 15." This way, the jury sees what's going on, again, because you've laid the groundwork.

Then you read the question, and you read it clearly, loudly, and slowly, so the witness, the jury, and everyone else hears it. "Question: How far away were you when you first saw something on the train tracks? And this was your answer. Answer: I was three..." Then I turn and look at a jury. "I was three car lengths away. Do you recall being asked that question and giving that answer?" The witness often says something like, "Oh, I may have..." or "I don't recall that." And if they don't recall it, you say, "Your Honor, I'd ask counsel to stipulate that that was a fair and accurate reading of the witness's answer under oath." And then, the judge says, "Counsel, any objection?" "No, that was it."

Next you say, "So a year ago, under oath, closer to the time of the accident, you didn't hesitate, you didn't approximate, you said three car lengths away. But now, for the first time, when I'm cross-examining you in front of this jury, you're now hedging and saying maybe one or two car lengths away. That's what you just said, isn't that right, sir?"

That's how you do it. That's how to impeach a witness.

You don't have to do it with precisely those words, but you do have to get the gist of it. They testified previously, under oath, with a lawyer there, answered truthfully, and now it's inconsistent.

When to impeach. If you're going to impeach, make sure you have something that's a direct contradiction. Many attorneys try to impeach my witnesses or other witnesses in other trials where there's really not an inconsistent statement. My witness will say, "Yeah, I walked to work that day." They'll say, "Do you recall giving a deposition on this date?" And they'll go through all the foundation questions to set up the impeachment. And I'll be thinking, "I don't know where they're going. I've looked through this transcript, and I know everything my client said." And then

85

the answer will be, "And your answer was, I walked to work, but it was later that day," or something like that. There's nothing inconsistent. It just looks weak, and the jury has no idea why they're doing it.

If you want to impeach, make sure it's on something important, it's strongly inconsistent, and you've locked them down. That way, you're keeping them in control. As you continue, if you get to a point where a witness is giving you a hard time, you can hold up the transcript and say, "Do we need to look back at your transcript? Remember what you said..." "Oh no, no, I remember." You're sort of waving the transcript at them.

You can use a similar strategy during your adversary's cross-examination, when you are choosing when to object. My recommendation is to object only when it's important. I once was in a trial with a seasoned defense attorney. His name was on the door of his law firm. He was the senior partner overseeing the case that the associate handled up until the time of trial. At the trial, while I was just doing background of my client on direct, I said something like, "Can you tell the jury where you live?" He said, "Objection, leading." And I said, "First of all, it wasn't leading. And second, why are you objecting to that?" And the judge, who wasn't a very skilled trial judge at the time, brought us into chambers to discuss what a leading question was. Don't object unless it's important and you have a legitimate basis for doing so.

Finishing Strong

We've covered how to prepare, digest, identify points, do your research, do the collateral work, move around the courtroom, feel comfortable with the question and answer, do the inflections, check out the jury, and cue them a little bit.

Then, when it's time to stop, stop. Don't stand up there and ask more questions because you're feeling good. You always want to end strong. Just as with direct-examination, never end on an objection sustained. You never want to ask a question, have there be an objection, have the judge sustain it, and say, "I have nothing further," unless you're doing it to make a point. You really want to think about what your last question will be on both direct and cross-examination.

In the case of this train operator, I could have had as my last question, "You could have stopped the train earlier, but you didn't, correct?" And that's a good question. Because there's nothing the witness is going to say. Then you end, and you say, "Thank you." As in all examinations and all presentations, whether it's opening or closing, you want to finish strong, take a deep breath, turn, and walk confidently back to the counsel table.

Even if the cross didn't go as well as you hoped, you want to appear strong. Maybe the jury will think it was good just because you looked like you were doing a good job, even if, substantively, you didn't get everything you wanted. Impressions are important. Always keep that in mind—jurors are looking at you all the time.

CHAPTER 4 APPENDIX

MY CROSS–EXAMINATION OF DEFENDANT'S EXPERT ACCIDENT RECONSTRUCTION EXPERT WITNESS IN OSCAR'S CASE

CROSS EXAMINATION BY MR. SMILEY:

Q. Good afternoon, Mr. G.

A. Good afternoon.

Q. Fair to say you are a man of science?

A. I hope so.

Q. When you come to a court of law like this, you come to talk about science, right?

A. I come to talk about -

THE COURT: Sir, I am going to ask now if the question requires a yes or no answer, simply answer yes or no without any editorializing. If there is an explanation required, they will present that, or you can give that afterwards based on a question, so just answer the questions yes or no if they are asked in that form. You may restate your question.

BY MR. SMILEY:

Q. When you come to a court of law like in a case like this, you come to bring your scientific expertise correct, sir?

A. Correct.

Q. And your opinion is only good upon the facts upon which your opinion is based?

A. Correct.

Q. Is it fair to say you do a fair amount of homework before you give an opinion to a jury?

A. Yes.

Q. And that involves taking measurements, right?

A. Yes.

Q. Taking photographs?

A. Yes.

Q. Doing your due diligence as far as inspections?

A. Yes.

Q. Let's talk about what you did and what you didn't do in this case.

I saw Defendant's Exhibit G, H and I which you purport are lines of sight, correct?

A. Yes.

Q. Those are only lines of sight that you purport that Oscar had as he looked up the roadway, correct?

A. Could you rephrase that please?

Q. Yes.

You only brought to this jury photographs that you created to purport to be a line of sight of Oscar A.'s view looking up in the direction of Carol L., correct?

A. Yes.

Q. You didn't also create line of sight diagrams for this jury to consider showing what Carol L.'s line of sight would be as she approached the intersection, did you?

A. It is the same thing.

Q. Well, you didn't show that line of sight going past

the intersection to see how far she could see, did you? THE COURT: It is a yes or no. THE WITNESS: I would have to qualify my answer. THE COURT: Okay.

Q. Sir, is it fair to say you did not create any diagram that shows the line of sight that Carol L. would have looking southbound beyond the intersection to see how far down Little Neck Parkway she could see for vehicles such as Oscar A. approaching that intersection, did you?

A. If you are looking for a yes or no, I have to qualify my answer.

Q. I am asking: If you created a diagram -

A. Same thing as the motorcycle can see.

THE COURT: Let me ask you this, sir: If you did

it only from Carol L., you would have to do it from the

point certain from Carol L. to observe moving forward;

would that be accurate?

THE WITNESS: I would have to qualify my answer,

your Honor. THE COURT: You can qualify your answer. THE WITNESS: May I have that exhibit, please? THE COURT: I am asking a question without the

exhibit.

If you were asked to determine the sight line

from a particular person, you would have to do that from a

set position?

THE WITNESS: Yes. THE COURT: And what position would you set it for Carol L.. THE WITNESS: The same position that I set it for the motorcycle in the opposite direction. THE COURT: Okay. BY MR. SMILEY:

Q. Did you take measurements of the Audi?

A. Yes.

Q. You -

A. I'm sorry. No, I did not take specific measurements of the Audi.

I have that - THE COURT: That's enough; yes or no.

A. No.

Q. When you went to go see the Audi, you didn't take any measurement, correct?

A. No. THE COURT: No, you didn't. THE WITNESS: I put my ruler in and took some

photographs.

THE COURT: Did you take measurements of the

Audi, yes or no?

THE WITNESS: I would have to qualify my answer,

your Honor.

THE COURT: What measurements did you take?

THE WITNESS: I put a ruler and took photographs,

so that's the measurements.

THE COURT: What measurements did you take?

THE WITNESS: They are in the photographs, your

Honor. THE COURT: Sir, tell me a measurement. I am not trying to be tricky. You took a measurement. Tell me what

the measurement was. THE WITNESS: I put a ruler in the photograph and

showed - THE COURT: And measured what? THE WITNESS: The front of the Audi. THE COURT: What were your measurements? THE WITNESS: I would have to look at the

photograph, your Honor. THE COURT: Your witness. BY MR. SMILEY:

Q. You measured the front of the Audi?

A. The height.

Q. And you have a photograph of that?

A. I don't think I have them in front of me here. I would have to see -

(Whereupon, there was a pause in the proceedings.)

A. I have a few pictures of the measurement that I took in front of the Audi.

Q. You didn't discuss the measurements in your direct, correct?

A. Excuse me?

Q. You didn't discuss any of those measurements in your direct examination?

A. I did not.

Q. Do you take any measurement at the location of the accident to determine how far the Audi was from the left side of Grand Central Parkway when it came to a complete stop?

A. No, I didn't.

Q. You didn't?

A. No.

Q. You didn't think that would be important?

A. I used the photograph.

Q. You didn't measure it though, did you?

A. No, I didn't know exactly where it was, so I used the photographs.

Q. For a scientific purpose to try to determine the width of room between the Audi and the side of the road, you don't have that measurement to use as part of forming your opinion, do you?

A. I don't have the specific measurement, but it is in the photograph.

Q. You don't have any measurement.

A. It is in the photograph. THE COURT: Sir, you have to just answer the

question. Either you took a measure or you didn't. THE WITNESS: No, I did not. THE COURT: Then that's the answer. You did not take a measurement? THE WITNESS: No.

BY MR. SMILEY:

Q. In fact, did you take any measurements regarding the position of the Audi at the location of the scene of the accident?

A. No.

Q. And when you testified earlier that where the Audi was stopped was one hundred feet from the entrance to the Grand Central Parkway, did you actually measure the front of that Audi to the front of the Grand Central Parkway to get one hundred feet?

A. I didn't - THE COURT: Yes or no?

A. No, I did not.

Q. But you told the Court that you did, right?

A. No, I told the Court that I estimated the distance based on car lengths from where the Audi was stopped to the entrance to the parkway.

Q. So you just stood there, sir. You took some photographs, and you figured in your mind and your expertise how long cars are and how many lanes and what that distance would be? You eyeballed it?

A. I didn't eyeball it. I took a ruler out, and I measured it and came up with approximately a hundred feet.

Q. Well, that's not science. Science is an actual measurement, right? You take out a ruler and you measure the length?

A. I just said I measured it with a ruler, and it is approximately one hundred feet.

Q. Where is that measurement? Do you have a picture of the ruler showing one hundred feet?

A. No, sir, I don't.

Q. That is just your recollection?

A. Yes.

Q. And you know coming into this case that there is a claim that the Audi struck the back of the motorcycle. You are aware that that is a claim in this case, right?

A. Yes.

Q. And, in fact, in the police report Oscar A. gives a statement to the police that is contained in Exhibit Ten that says he was struck by the Audi, right?

A. Correct.

Q. And Carol L. has a statement in that police report that says the vehicles collided, correct?

A. Correct.

Q. And as a scientist, it is important for you to consider that in coming to this Court in front of this jury and giving your opinion, correct?

A. I would have to qualify my answer. THE COURT: Yes or no. THE WITNESS: I can't answer it yes or no.

Q. Well, you have to consider that?

A. I would have to qualify my answer.

Q. Did you consider the statements within the police report that her vehicle either struck Oscar A. or their vehicles collided? Did you consider that, yes or no?

A. I did.

Q. All right.

Now knowing that there was a claim that they either collided or that the Audi struck the motorcycle, sir, didn't you think it would be important to take a look at that motorcycle?

A. I did.

Q. And did you take any steps to go and actually look at that motorcycle?

A. I requested to examine the motorcycle.

Q. And what happened to that request?

A. I was told I wasn't allowed.

Q. Who told you you weren't allowed?

A. I don't recall specifically who told me.

Q. Okay.

MR. SMILEY: Let the record reflect, for the record, as an officer of the Court there was no request by anyone to have Mr. A.'s motorcycle inspected by this witness.

Q. Now, it is important in a case like this if you are going to come and testify to this jury to have that kind of inspection, isn't it?

A. Yes --excuse me.

Q. It is important in a case like this if you are going to come in as an expert for the defense to have inspected the motorcycle personally, isn't it?

A. I think it would. I can't answer it yes or no. I would have to qualify my answer.

Q. I don't want you to qualify your answers, sir.

A. I would have to qualify my answer in this question.

Q. Did you think it would be important for you to physically look at the motorcycle before coming today to testify in front of this jury?

A. It would have been helpful.

Q. Because if you looked at it, you could have taken measurements, correct?

A. I could have.

Q. You could have measured the height of the right rear saddle bags, correct?

A. I could have.

Q. You could have compared that to the height of the front fender. You said you measured the front fender?

A. I did.

Q. And you have no reason to dispute that the front fender of the Audi lines up perfectly with the right saddle bag?

A. That's a very difficult question to answer. I am not sure where on the Audi the saddle back would line up to.

Q. You don't know that because you didn't measure.

A. There are differences of height along the front of the Audi.

Q. Do you have -

A. When I looked at the Audi, I didn't see any marks on the Audi to correspond to where the area of the motorcycle is alleged to have had contact.

Q. That's what the --what I am asking. I am asking if you had measurements --had taken measurements of the Audi and the saddle bag, you could compare the height of the saddle bag to the front of the Audi; couldn't you have done that?

A. I did that.

Q. Tell us what the measurements were of the saddle bag of the motorcycle.

A. I would have to look at the picture of the motorcycle to tell you what the height of the saddle bags are.

Q. Go ahead.

A. Give me an exhibit.

Q. How can you measure a motor vehicle's sight?

A. Where is the ruler there?

Q. I haven't seen any ruler in the back of the motorcycle, sir. I am not asking what is in your binder. I am asking what is in evidence.

A. Well, are you asking me to show you this picture with

the ruler? THE COURT: Take the picture down, sir. See, this trial is about what is in evidence in

this trial. I don't know what you looked at, sir. I am just telling you how I conduct a trial. Next question. BY MR. SMILEY:

Q. Now isn't it true, sir, you are not really coming in here as an objective expert in this case? Isn't that true?

A. You are looking for a yes or a no, or do you want to me to answer the question?

Q. Looking for a yes or no.

A. I am completely objective in the work that I do.

Q. All right.

Now, if you were objective, you wouldn't have anything to do with the work you have done previously for Mr. D.'s law firm, would it?

A. I am not sure I understand.

Q. You have testified for his law firm before today, haven't you?

A. I have.

Q. On many occasions, haven't you?

A. Yes.

Q. How many occasions?

A. I don't know that number specifically.

THE COURT: How about approximately?

Q. Ballpark it.

A. Fifteen maybe.

Q. Fifteen times? Mr. D. called you to testify in a courtroom like

this on behalf of his defendant client, correct?

MR. D.: Objection.

THE COURT: Basis.

MR. D.: It never happened.

THE COURT: He never testified -

MR. D.: Not me --not me.

THE COURT: --fifteen times for your firm?

MR. D.: That I can't say. I can't represent

that. He said, "Mr. D."

MR. SMILEY: I will rephrase.

THE COURT: Let's not play with this.

Have you testified on behalf of the plaintiff's

firm -

MR. SMILEY: Defendant.

THE COURT: --defendant's firm approximately

fifteen times? THE WITNESS: Previously, yes, your Honor; not for Mr. D. THE COURT: Understood. BY MR. SMILEY:

Q. Do you know the name of his law firm?

A. Yes.

Q. What is that?

A. P. and S.

Q. When did you first start testifying in a courtroom on behalf of P. and S.?

A. I don't recall the year.

Q. Because it was that long ago?

A. No, I just don't recall the year.

Q. Fair to say at least ten years ago is when you first started testifying for the firm?

A. It is possible.

Q. Isn't it likely?

A. I said, "It is possible."

Q. Each of those times they pay you, sir, to come testify, right?

A. That's correct.

Q. They pay you before trial to do your analysis, correct?

A. Yes, sir.

Q. And how much have they paid you in this case before trial?

A. Probably six to seven thousand dollars.

Q. And how much have they paid you to come to testify here in court?

A. About three thousand dollars.

Q. About ten thousand dollars?

A. Correct.

Q. For that they don't even get a diagram from you to

show this jury, correct? MR. D.: Objection.

A. I don't understand.

THE COURT: You have to stand for your objection, and your objection is overruled.

Q. You didn't bring a diagram showing the analysis that --that you prepared to explain to this jury what happened in this case objectively, did you?

A. I did not make a diagram, correct.

Q. That's something that is normally done by accident reconstructionists?

A. Not necessarily.

Q. It would be helpful?

A. In this case I didn't think it was necessary.

Q. And on the fifteen times prior that you testified for P. and S., the fees were about the same in those cases?

A. It varies.

Q. Approximately ten thousand dollars a pop?

A. Not necessarily.

Q. And there are cases that they have retained you on to analyze and review and they paid you that don't go to trial?

A. That's correct.

Q. About how many of those cases have you done for Mr. D.'s law firm?

A. I don't know that number.

Q. More than twenty?

A. Yes.

Q. More than fifty?

A. Probably between fifty to one hundred.

Q. So between fifty to one hundred cases that they paid you to review that didn't go to trial, correct?

A. Correct.

Q. And about fifteen or so that they paid you to come and testify at trial?

A. That's probably accurate.

Q. Would it be a reasonable statement for me to make that as of today you have received consulting job work that you have done for the law firm of P & S you have made over one hundred thousand dollars easily?

A. Over the last ten years I would say that's probably accurate.

Q. Maybe two hundred thousand dollars?

A. I don't know what that number is.

Q. You have done quite well working for them. MR. D.: Objection.

THE COURT: Sustained.

Question answer stricken from the record.

Direct the jury to disregard. BY MR. SMILEY:

Q. Now, let's see what else you did to give an objective opinion to this Court.

Did you hear any evidence or were you provided any evidence today at this trial to support any opinion that Oscar A. just fell without any impact?

THE COURT: That's a yes or a no.

A. Did I hear any evidence that he just fall without an impact?

Q. Yes.

A. From testimony? Previous testimony?

Q. No.

I am asking about any evidence in this courtroom that you could point us to or any hypothetical that Mr. D. gave you as part of your opinion today that supports any opinion based on the fact that he just fell?

A. I am not understanding your question. You want me to give my opinion as to what I think happened?

Q. No, sir.

I am asking: What, if any, evidence is there scientifically that his motorcycle just fell without any contact?

A. The evidence that I pointed out on my previous testimony which I will be happy to explain again.

Q. Specifically, what evidence that it just fell without any contact?

A. There's a couple of photographs that show the mark on the ground and where the position of where the Audi is that, in my opinion, clearly indicates that it fell as it was moving ahead of the Audi.

Q. That's your objective opinion?

A. That's my opinion, your Honor --counsel.

Q. Now, you say that the motorcycle is thirty-six inches wide from handlebar to handlebar?

A. That's the width of the handlebars, the estimated width of the handlebars.

Q. There is no evidence that the handlebars of his car had any contact with the Audi, is there?

A. I didn't see any evidence of contact, no.

Q. How wide are his motorcycle tires?

A. Typically motorcycle tires are approximately four inches.

Q. How wide was the space at the time that you think that Mr. A. passed Mrs. L.? How wide a space was there between her car and the left side of the roadway?

A. My estimate would be about five feet.

Q. Plenty of room to go by on a motorcycle, right?

A. I think it's a little bit narrow because that only leaves you with about twelve inches on either side of the vehicle. So my opinion, that's narrow.

Q. Why would he fall if he had four to five feet of room? The tires are only four inches. Why wasn't there enough room?

A. I think it is a very narrow distance between the driver's side of the Audi, and this is an estimate. It could have been less; and if it was less, again, it would explain why he fell to the ground.

Q. You are still not explaining why there is not enough room, scientifically, for him to get by.

A. I don't feel comfortable driving my vehicle with less than a foot on either side of it. When you are going through something --if you are moving between a truck and a curb, and you have only twelve inches on either side, you gotta take precautions. You can't move fast, and in my opinion the vehicle was going faster than the Audi in a very narrow circumstance and that's what caused him to fall.

Q. Do you claim to be an expert in the operation of motorcycles?

A. No. I claim be an expert in -

Q. That's a yes or no.

A. I would have to qualify that answer.

Q. Do you claim to be an expert in the operation of

motorcycles?

A. I would have to qualify.

Q. Can you answer yes or no?

A. I will repeat myself. I would have to qualify my answer.

Q. Do you have a motorcycle license?

A. No.

Q. Can't be an expert in driving a motorcycle when you don't have a motorcycle license, correct?

A. I would have to qualify that answer.

Q. Okay.

Now, you --you were talking about the speed that you claim that Mr. A. passed Mrs. L.'s vehicle. You say he was going faster than her?

A. Yes.

Q. You how fast was he going?

A. I don't know.

Q. You have no idea?

A. I have no idea of how fast he was going at the time he lost control of his vehicle.

Q. No idea?

A. No. I would be estimating it.

Q. Well, isn't that part of why you are here, sir, to reconstruct the accident? If you are going to give an opinion to this jury in this very serious matter that he was going faster than her, and he was going so fast that he lost control of his motorcycle, don't you think, scientifically, you should tell this jury how fast he was going with a reasonable degree of scientific certainty?

A. Are you looking for a yes or no, or do you want me qualify my answer?

Q. Yes or no.

Don't you think you should be able to tell the jury that?

A. Let me qualify my answer.

Q. Yes or no.

A. Let me qualify my answer.

Q. Did you take steps to determine the speed of Mr. A.'s vehicle at the time that you believe he was passing Mrs. L.'s car?

A. I didn't have enough physical evidence for me to give a precise speed of the motorcycle. I can give an estimate because I know how he accelerated. And I know roughly how fast the Audi was going. I don't think he was going in an excessive rate of speed, but given the conditions he was traveling in, it is very difficult.

Q. That's a lot of information to opine on based on just looking at the photographs, isn't it?

A. It is not just the photographs. You have to look at evidence when you look at the photographs, and you go to the scene and evaluate it.

Q. So, do you know where the motorcycle came to rest?

A. Specifically no. There are no pictures that indicate that, but you see where the tire --the scrap mark ends, so you can get an estimate as to where the motorcycle came to rest.

Q. I am not talking about estimates.

Scientifically, weren't there steps, sir, that you could have taken, had you chosen to do so, to come to this jury and scientifically show them where you believe the motorcycle came to a rest in the roadway? Couldn't you have done that?

A. I would be happy to show you where the motorcycle came to rest.

Q. Well, you didn't show us, did you?

A. Sure, I did.

Give me one of those exhibits, and I will show you where the scrap mark ends, and that's where the motorcycle came to rest.

Q. How far was it in feet was that from the front of the Audi vehicle when it came to stop?

A. If I have to estimate, it would be fifteen feet or so.

Q. That's not very scientific, is it?

A. This is not a scientific field, counsel. This is an estimate of science. It's an approximation. It is not like DNA or fingerprints. You make estimations. It is not a precise scientific field, not like DNA or fingerprints. An analyst in this field makes estimations.

Q. So you are saying you couldn't create a scale diagram, place the vehicles where you believe the evidence showed they were, show the distances, show where the Audi came to rest and where the motorcycle came to the rest? You couldn't do that for this jury?

A. I have perfect pictures to show you.

Q. That's not my question.

A. Then I have to qualify my answer. THE COURT: The question is: Could you have done

that, sir? That's a yes or no.

A. I could have done that. THE COURT: If you just answer the question -

everything can't be qualified. You could have done it was the answer. Next question.

Q. Now, you said you looked at the photographs of the motorcycle and the only damage you saw was a scrap mark on the bar of the motor vehicle?

A. Well, you want this as a yes or a no?

Q. Yes. MR. D.: Objection, your Honor. THE COURT: Come up.

(Whereupon, there was an off-the-record discussion held in the robing room.) THE COURT: I am going to ask you to rephrase your question. BY MR. SMILEY:

Q. Sir, did you see damage to Oscar A.'s motorcycle when you reviewed the photographs in evidence?

A. I did.

Q. Where did you see damage to his motorcycle?

A. Predominantly the scrap marks on the left side.

Q. Where else?

A. That was the most significant damage that I noted. THE COURT: The question is not "significant." You said "predominantly." Where else did you see damage?

The jury and the Court are trying to get answers to the question, so when you say "predominantly," where else did you see damage?

A. I saw damage on the left side of the motorcycle.

Q. And the damage you saw --the only damage you saw was to the bar on the left side of the motorcycle?

A. Yes.

Q. Do you see damage anywhere else to his motorcycle as a result of this accident?

A. No.

Q. Did you look closely?

A. Yes.

Q. Now, when you went to the scene --the location to do a site inspection and you take some photographs, did you mark the pavement at all to try to line up the actual locations of where the scratch mark was?

A. No.

Q. Did you take any measurements that were photographed so the jury can see specific measurements you took?

A. No.

Q. Did you create a scale diagram of the accident location?

A. No.

Q. These are all things you could have done, correct?

A. Correct.

Q. Before going to look at the Audi, you were aware that there was no claim of damage to the Audi, correct?

A. Possibly; I don't recall specifically.

Q. And it is no surprise to you that a collision like this could occur where the front of an Audi hits the right rear saddle bag of a motorcycle and there be no scratch on the Audi? That could happen, right?

A. I suppose that's a possibility.

Q. I am sure in the thousands of accident reconstructions you have done over the last forty years there have been instances where vehicles have collided and one of the vehicles shows no damage, correct?

A. That's possible.

Q. Well, it's likely, isn't it?

A. I said it is "possible."

Q. And the Audi involved in this case --you know the model number, right?

A. Yes.

Q. And you know what year it was, right?

A. Yes.

Q. What year was it? THE WITNESS: May I look at my notes, your Honor? THE COURT: Absolutely. (Whereupon, there was a pause in the

proceedings.) A. 2013.

Q. Now, you use something called, um, Expert Auto Stats to determine specifications for the car --did you do that?

A. Yes.

Q. And what year did you get the expert auto stats for the Audi?

A. A 2012 on the Audi stats.

Q. You didn't do the 2013, right?

A. I did it on another program.

Q. You didn't do it on the auto stats, right?

A. No.

Q. The one on the other program that's also showing 2012 statistics on this Audi, right?

A. Well, it comes up model year 2013.

Q. Do you know if that one that you are just referring to now that says 2012 and also talks about 2013, that's referring to the defendant's car? Are you sure about that?

A. Yeah, the VIN number matches, so that's what it came up with.

Q. Why would you use a report of a 2012 instead of a 2013 vehicles?

A. That's what I printed out.

Q. How long was the scrap mark on the concrete?

A. I don't know specifically. I said, looking at the photographs, I estimate it possibly about fifteen feet.

Q. You didn't measure it, right?

A. No.

Q. You could have measured it, right?

A. It wasn't there when I went there.

Q. You could have used methods --scientific methods to determine the length of the --that mark, couldn't you have?

A. Yes, I could have.

Q. But you didn't, did you?

A. No.

MR. SMILEY: Can we please show the witness Exhibit Three?

(Whereupon, there was a pause in the proceedings.) BY MR. SMILEY:

Q. Okay.

Now, sir, you know what this shows on Exhibit Three - what view this is?

A. Yes.

Q. Are you aware at some point this would have been the approximate view of Carol L. as she was approaching Grand Central Parkway Service Road to turn right, right?

A. Yes.

Q. How far of a line did she have looking down Little Neck Parkway from this perspective? How far could she see if there were no cars in this photograph?

A. Several hundred feet.

Q. Two hundred?

A. At least, minimum.

Q. Four hundred?

A. Perhaps.

Q. Five hundred?

A. I would say probably about five hundred. That's an estimate.

Q. Did you take the measurement?

A. No.

Q. Did you do your Google map thing where you took that photograph, and you put a line here, and you shot the line down Little Neck Parkway so you could come to tell this jury what Carol L.'s line of sight would have been looking down to see if she could have seen any vehicles before entering that intersection?

A. From this point here, counsel?

Q. Yes.

A. No, not at all.

Q. That would have been helpful, wouldn't it have?

A. Not at all.

Q. Well, how far down should Carol L. have been able to see Oscar A. if he was up in the roadway?

A. At this point here?

Q. Yeah.

A. Without any cars?

Q. Yeah.

A. So no cars on the road except the Audi and the motor vehicle?

Q. Yeah.

A. How far down she could see?

Q. Yeah.

A. Whatever estimate I said, five hundred feet.

Q. There is no reason she shouldn't have seen him before the accident, right?

A. You want me to assume how far down she could see a motorcycle approach?

Q. Yeah.

A. Maybe five hundred feet.

Q. My question is, sir: There is no reason why she, Carol L., should not have been able to see Oscar A. before she made that right-hand turn assuming --assuming what you have been assuming, that he came up and passed her?

A. I am not sure I understand your question.

Q. Let's assume for the moment what you have been testifying that you believe that she made the turn and Oscar came and passed her, okay?

A. Correct.

Q. How far back on the Little Neck Parkway would he have had to have been at the point where she is about to make this right-hand turn?

A. I have no idea.

Q. No idea?

A. How am I going to know what his speed is if he is stopping for a light? If he is accelerating? Decelerating? No possible way to scientifically analyze that.

Q. Is it fair to say because she had several hundred feet in your explanation --wherever it was --she should have seen him?

A. I don't know where he is. I don't know if there are cars, so I don't know what your question is.

Q. All right.

I want you to assume that Carol L. testified as she approaching to make the right-hand turn, she looked down Little Neck Parkway, this view, sees no northbound traffic, okay?

A. Okay.

Q. I want you to further assume Carol L.'s version that he came out of nowhere and passed her on the left, and this accident occurred, okay?

A. Okay.

Q. Based on those two assumptions, shouldn't she have seen him coming northbound on Little Neck Parkway before the turn?

A. I think it is a possibility.

Q. Shouldn't she have, not a possibility? We are talking science here.

A. No, we are not talking science, counsel. I said I think it is possible.

Q. Within a reasonable degree of scientific certainty wouldn't she have seen him?

A. I said it is possible.

Q. Well -

A. That's my answer.

Q. Well, if he is - THE COURT: Let me ask you the question

differently: If she was positioned there, based upon all of

your calculations and speed and whatever, would the

motorcycle be in her sight line?

That's a yes or a no.

THE WITNESS: It's possible.

THE COURT: It is not --sight line is not a

possibility.

As an accident reconstructionist, would not any

position down that road be in her sight line?

That's a yes or a no.

THE WITNESS: Yes; it could be, yes. BY MR. SMILEY:

Q. It is not that hard to just say "yes." MR. D.: Objection. THE COURT: Sustained.

Q. Just to be clear for this jury, if there is(sic) no other cars coming northbound, based on your analysis of this accident, before she made that right turn, Carol L. should have seen Oscar A. on his motorcycle; isn't that true, sir?

A. I would say could have.

Q. You won't acknowledge it? THE COURT: Let's move on.

Q. How fast would Oscar A. have to have been traveling on his motorcycle for Carol L. not to see him before the turn because he is not far away, made the turn and Oscar come up, catch up on her, and, as you claim, pass her on the left? How fast did he have to be driving?

A. I can't answer that question. I don't know where he is on the road. I don't know how fast he is going as he is coming up. I can't answer that question.

Q. Do you even know what the difference in speed was at the time of this incident between the two vehicles? MR. D.: Objection. THE COURT: Overruled. It is a yes or no.

A. No.

Q. Do you know how it was, based on your analysis, that Oscar A. fell --how his motorcycle actually fell? How did it go from being upright and straight to down on the ground?

A. Do I know how it happened or why?

Q. How.

A. I don't know how --I know how it happened, yes. He went down on the ground on the left side of the vehicle.

Q. Okay.

How did that happen? How did he go from riding on his motorcycle to all of a sudden being on his left side down on the ground?

A. Because he is traveling too fast for a narrow condition.

Q. Well, if it is as narrow as you claim, you don't know the measurement, and he fell to the left, wouldn't he have fallen off the roadway onto the grass to the left there?

A. I don't know --he fell. Obviously, he fell in front of Audi because of the mark.

Q. Sir, did you run any analysis based upon the potential for evidence in this trial to show that there was a collision between the Audi and the motorcycle?

A. Define analysis.

Q. Do you calculate where the vehicles would end up? Where the sight lines would be? What speeds they would have been at? Where they started at? Where they ended at based on the actual collision?

A. I can testify as to how I thought this accident occurred which is what I thought I did.

Q. That's not what I am asking.

The only analysis that you performed was based upon your claim that there was no contact between the vehicles, correct?

A. There is no evidence --no physical forensic evidence in my opinion to indicate that the front of the Audi contacted the back of the motorcycle.

Q. And that's based on your -

A. That's my analysis, counsel.

Q. Your analysis of looking at the back of the motorcycle, right?

A. That's my analysis looking at all the evidence I have discussed, examining the Audi and looking at the pictures of the motorcycle.

Q. My question, sir, is different.

My question: Did you perform any reconstruction based upon the potential for evidence in this trial coming out that there was a collision between the two vehicles? Did you attempt to reconstruct this evidence based upon a collision of the two vehicles?

A. Yes.

There is a nine page report in my report that indicates my reconstruction. It is a nine page report of my analysis.

MR. SMILEY: Objection. Move to strike. THE COURT: Overruled.

Q. Do you present this jury with any analysis based upon a collision?

A. Absolutely.

It is a nine page report that I turned over to counsel.

Q. I am not asking what you gave to your lawyer. I am asking what you gave to this jury. Did you give them any analysis based on a collision of the two vehicles? THE COURT: Today?

MR. SMILEY: Today.

A. No; I didn't, no.

Q. Are you aware, sir, that there was testimony at this trial that there was a collision between these two vehicles?

A. I'm aware.

Q. Even though you are aware that there is evidence in this case that the two vehicles collided, you were unable to come and testify to this jury about a reconstruction of this accident based upon a collision, weren't you?

A. You would have to define the word "evidence," please.

Q. I don't have to define that for you.

THE COURT: Okay, this is not --both gentlemen, this not a debate, so next question.

Q. Knowing that there is information of a collision between these two vehicles --and you knew that from the police report, right?

A. Yes.

Q. Did you come objectively prepared to discuss how this accident could have occurred based upon a collision of these vehicles?

A. I did, yes.

Q. And what is your opinion if there was a collision of the speed of the vehicles at the time of the collision?

A. You want --I am not sure I understand that. Rephrase that.

MR. D.: Objection, your Honor. THE COURT: Overruled. MR. D.: Two questions.

A. What is the question?

Q. So you did an analysis based on a collision?

A. No, I did an analysis based on the evidence that I examined.

Q. My question is: I want you to assume there is evidence in this case the defendant --she testified, I may have hit him, okay? Our vehicles may have collided. You know from the police report it talks about a collision, being struck, right?

A. Yes.

Q. Did you take that information and do an accident reconstruction, based on a collision between the two vehicles to then be able to explain to this jury what you believe occurred leading up to those events to cause a collision? Did you do that analysis?

A. I am --you would have to please rephrase the question because I am confused as to -

THE COURT: Let me try this.

MR. SMILEY: Thank you.

THE COURT: Did you exclude any possibility of the contact between the vehicle and the motorcycle? THE WITNESS: Your Honor -

THE COURT: That's a yes or no. THE WITNESS: Where on the vehicle, your Honor? THE COURT: You are saying there was no contact. THE WITNESS: I am saying in my opinion - THE COURT: No, sir. I am asking a specific question: Did you take in consideration at all that there was contact?

THE WITNESS: I can't rule out incidental contact between the right side of the motorcycle and the driver's side of the Audi as the motorcycle is moving up alongside the Audi. I can't rule that out. Maybe there was incidental contact. I didn't see any evidence of that but maybe there was.

BY MR. SMILEY:

Q. Where was that incidental contact?

A. I just said it.

Q. Where?

A. Where what? I just testified to that.

Q. Between the vehicles; where would that incidental contact have been?

A. I said if --if there was any incidental contact, it occurred with the right side of the motorcycle and the driver's side of the Audi when the motorcycle was moving up into that narrow space --if.

THE COURT: Okay.

That's move on. We are not --let's proceed with a different line of questioning at this point. BY MR. SMILEY:

Q. Where was the motorcycle when Carol L. made her right turn onto Grand Central Parkway?

A. I don't believe, in my opinion, that it was on the service road yet.

Q. Where was it?

A. Making its turn after the Audi was already on the service road.

Q. Did it start to make its turn?

A. What? The motorcycle or the Audi?

Q. The motorcycle. Did it start to make its turn when she made her turn?

A. I think the motorcycle made its turn after the Audi was on the service road.

Q. Okay.

Now, can you tell this jury specifically where that motorcycle was when the Audi made its turn?

A. No.

Q. What was the position of the motorcycle prior to it going down to the ground into a skid? What was the orientation of the motorcycle?

A. Obviously, it had to be upright.

Q. Was it straight? Was it angled one way or the other?

A. I have no idea.

Q. You have no idea?

A. There is no way for me to determine that.

Q. Wouldn't the position of the motorcycle result in a different position that it would end up after the incident occurred when it went down?

A. I don't understand your question.

Q. If the motorcycle is angled to the right in front of her car and an impact occurred, would you expect it to end up coming to rest in the same position as if the motorcycle was straight when it was hit?

A. There are many factors there that I can't answer that question. MR. SMILEY: Now can we please show Exhibit Six to the witness?

THE COURT: Yes.

Come up. (Whereupon, there was an off-the-record discussion held in the robing room.)

BY MR. SMILEY:

Q. I would like to wrap it up because we are at the end of the court date, sir.

Finally, was there any consideration in your mind of how to present your accident reconstruction to this jury based upon the claim that these two vehicles collided, or was your sole analysis based on your premise that they didn't touch each other?

THE COURT: Compound question.

I am going to ask you to rephrase.

Q. Was your sole analysis that you gave this jury based upon your premise that there is no contact between those vehicles?

THE WITNESS: I would have to qualify that, your Honor.

Q. I don't want you to qualify. Can you answer the question, yes or no?

A. I can't sir.

MR. SMILEY: All right. I have no further questions.

CHAPTER 5

CLOSING ARGUMENTS

In this chapter, you'll learn how to prepare for and present your closing argument, also known as the summation, which is at the end of the trial once the witness examinations are complete. It's an exciting part of the trial. Other than the opening statement, it's the only time you control the content and delivery of what the jury hears. As much as we try to control the content of our direct and cross-examinations, there are unpredictable witnesses, adversaries objecting, unknowns, and X factors out of our control that can influence the jury.

But in a summation, like an opening, you have the jury—your audience—sitting there. They want to hear from you. They want to listen to what you have to say about what transpired in this trial, and you need to deliver. This is your time to be creative, to be persuasive, and to put together all the bits and pieces of the trial that support your theory of the case. You need to deliver your summation to the jury in a way that will sink in. You want them to think about what they have seen and heard throughout the trial, and highlight significant points they may not have noticed during the trial. You may have elicited some great information from a witness in one of your examinations that helps make your case. What they said could align perfectly with the judge's charge, but the jury may not have caught it. In your summation, you can deliver it to them.

I am a plaintiff's lawyer, so over the last several decades, I've only given summations on behalf of plaintiffs in personal injury, wrongful death and medical malpractice cases. I've never presented a defense summation, although I've sat through many of them. For those of you on the defense side, it's crucial to see what goes through the preparation for a plaintiff's summation since that helps you to prepare for your defense.

The order of summations is almost always the defense first and the plaintiff last. Typically, the party with the burden of proof in a case goes first in openings and last in summations. Federal cases could be different, but most federal judges still follow that format.

Prior to summations, usually after both parties have rested their case, you'll have a charging conference with the trial judge. That's where you go over the law, the Pattern Jury Instructions (PJI) and what the jury will be charged with. After the summations are completed, the judge will charge the jury on the law. And then the jury deliberates the fate of your case.

Good Preparation Is Crucial

As in every other aspect of the trial, preparation is critical. It is the key to every element of the case, especially the summation. And preparing for your summation often starts before the actual trial even begins.

I almost always start thinking about how to address things in opening and summation well ahead of time. If you haven't started earlier, you certainly need to start preparing for your summation at the beginning of the trial. It begins with what you covered in your opening statement and goes through your examinations. I previously shared the analogy of picking "apples" for your summation. The apples are the items you need to obtain and establish through testimony and evidence to prove your case.

As a plaintiff, to make it to a jury, and not have your case dismissed as a matter of law, you must make out a *prima facie* case. If you're defending a case, you must establish the elements of your defense, or prove that the plaintiff was unable to meet their burden. The burden shifts from the plaintiff to the defense to prove the affirmative defenses, such as the plaintiff's comparative fault. So, you want to make sure that legally, you've done your job, and you've elicited the necessary evidence to support your side of the case. You want to make sure that you've collected your apples—your evidence—that will be persuasive in helping you win your case in front of the jury.

If you see a great summation, it's not because the lawyer is just getting up and winging it off the top of their head. It's because that lawyer has worked hard to prepare the content and organization of the summation prior to its delivery. There's a lot of behind-the-scenes work that goes into a summation. You need to take time. You may think, "What happens when you've been trying a case for days, weeks, or even months, and you're working late to prepare for the next day?

How do you have the time to prepare properly for summation?" The key is to take the time to organize and plan.

I suggest you keep a "trial notes" folder with you every day at trial. When something happens at trial, good or bad, you should take notes, then stick those notes in your folder. You can look at all those trial notes when it comes time to prepare for your summation.

Don't be shy about asking the judge what the schedule looks like as you get close to the end of the trial. During trials, there's a lot of downtime when the jury is not in the courtroom when you're talking with your adversary and the judge about what's coming up the next day and where you stand with the presentation of witnesses. As you're getting towards the end of the trial, you can ask the judge, "Your Honor, I want to make sure I have time to prepare properly. Do we have a schedule for the charging conference? When are you thinking we will present our summations?"

As it's getting much closer and you're deciding when to have the charging conference, you could say, "Your Honor, I would like to have some time to prepare for summations. Could we perhaps sum up Monday morning, so I have the weekend to prepare? Or perhaps we could do the charge conference Thursday morning and have Thursday afternoon off?" There's nothing wrong with asking. And I've only had one federal judge who didn't give me any time. I find most judges will be accommodating. If they won't, you'll need to work with what you have, but at least you asked.

How to Prepare for Your Summation

I'll walk you through my process for mapping it out. The key is to be organized. When you have time allotted to work on your summation, start by finding a quiet place. Don't sit in a busy office or in the middle of your kitchen where your family members are running around. Find a place in your office, in a room in your house, or somewhere else where you can tell everyone, "I'm locking myself in here to work on my summation. Nobody interrupt me."

My father used to do that all the time. In the house where I grew up, we had a room we called the sunroom. It was a three-season room with a lot of windows. He would tell us, "I'm going to the sunroom to prepare for trial (or summation, or for court the next day)." We all knew to leave him alone. We'd see him in there with his yellow legal pads and file contents spread all over.

91

That's what you want—a command center where you can bring all your files and trial notes, sit down, and start mapping out your summation.

Gather the dailies you need. I request daily transcripts, or transcripts of specific witnesses, from the court reporter as the trial proceeds. There's a court reporter for every trial, and it's usually the same person for the whole trial. Make friends with that court reporter. They know lawyers like dailies. You can tell them, "I want the daily of this witness," or, "I want dailies of all the testimony each day." My preference is to request specific dailies. They will email it to you that night. It's a bit expensive, but worth it.

In Oscar's case, I ordered the dailies of the defendant driver and owner of the car involved, as well as the defense reconstruction expert. I enjoy reading the dailies of my cross-examinations so that I can see the exact responses I elicited from adverse witnesses. Then I used those dailies when preparing for my summation. Digest the daily transcripts in the same manner discussed in Chapter 4, Cross-Examination. Go through the dailies and find the good answers that help your case. You can email the pages containing those answers to your exhibit specialist, who can make a nice big blow-up of the page for you to show the jury in your summation.

Summation is all about being persuasive. It's not only what you say to the jury. It's about what exhibits you have, which are the important pieces of evidence from the trial. It's also about testimony. You are entitled to blow up and share any testimony elicited during the trial. I often say, "Don't take my word for what this witness said. I printed it out, just to make sure that we're all on the same page. Here is exactly what this witness said on the stand when I asked this question. Let's look at it." And I show the enlargement of the testimony right there. I find that's a successful technique.

How to Create Your Outline

Once you have your dailies and trial notes, you can start working on your outline. For reference, I have included my summation outline for Oscar's case as Appendix-1 to this chapter. To recap, Oscar was on a motorcycle, turning left to get onto the Little Neck Parkway. The defendant was driving a car owned by her husband, and she was turning right to get onto the Little

Neck Parkway on an entrance ramp. They both went at the same time, there was an accident, and my client was severely injured.

This was a liability-only trial, so the summation I prepared for was for liability only and did not address damages or ask for compensation. When a trial is *bifurcated*, as opposed to unified, you try liability first. It's a full trial on liability. If the defendant is found liable, then you proceed to a full trial on damages. If it's a *unified* trial, with both liability and damages, everything goes into one summation. So, my notes here are for a liability trial only. But the preparation is the same for both.

Decide on an organization system. I love using a yellow pad. It might be a bit old school—I know many attorneys prefer to use their laptops. Whatever works for you. But whatever method you use, you must be organized. In this process, you won't hit it out of the park the first time you write everything out. It's the process that gets to what you want to talk about. So, you want to put your thoughts on paper, or on a computer.

Your order of presentation. The first thing to do is get an idea of the order. How do you want to present your summation? You can't just willy-nilly jump from point to point, because a jury won't follow you. You need to present your summation in a way that flows. Sometimes it's chronologically, sometimes, you go through the witnesses, and sometimes you go through your case, then you address the other side's case.

In my outline (Appendix-1), you will see I started with my regular introduction, then went over my theme. And then I wanted to cover what the defendants had just finished talking about, since their case goes on right before summations, after I've presented the plaintiff's case. I had a lot I wanted to say about the defendants' case, particularly what I thought were lies or shady things that came out in the defendant driver's testimony.

Key points to revisit. The defense had a reconstruction expert. I beat him up on my cross, and I wanted to hammer him in my summation. I had my trial notes about their expert and all the money he's made—over half a million dollars just from this defense firm alone. I wanted to talk about the difference between their expert, and our expert, who came in with science and diagrams and made more sense out of what an expert is supposed to bring to a jury and how it lines up with what the plaintiff said.

The verdict sheet. Next, I get to the verdict sheet. You will see that I'll put something in red ink or underline it in red when I think it's important. I also put the exhibits I want to show to the jury in red. That way, they jump out at me as I'm going through the preparation process. Also, if I need to look at my notes at some point during the trial, this outline will become my safety net. When it came time to deliver my summation, I didn't read one page of this or even look at it. I was engaged with the jury.

A standard opening. After that, I start to write out my summation. I always start with, "May it please the court." You need to have a routine to get your courtroom legs and to feel comfortable, so you don't get up there and draw a blank in front of a jury. You never want that to happen.

Start with your strong point. After the judge tells me to proceed, I address the jury. In this case, I said, "I hit a motorcycle." And I let it sink in, and then I said it again. "'I hit a motorcycle.' Those were the words the defendant spoke to her husband from the accident scene. 'I hit a motorcycle.' But she wouldn't say those same words when she swore to tell the truth in this courtroom. She wasn't straight with you, members of the jury." That's how I kicked off my summation.

You have your intro and then whatever strong point you have. In this case, that's, "I hit a motorcycle." At the deposition, the defendant's husband was asked, "Did she call you from the scene? What did she say?" And he replied, "She said, 'I hit a motorcycle.'" I knew that was going to be something strong to work with at trial.

I said, "She admitted it. But she didn't admit it to you. She admitted it to her husband. At trial, her testimony was, 'Well, I don't know, maybe I was cut off. I think he may have lost control.' She didn't say to her husband, 'I may have hit, or he may have lost control.' She said, 'I hit a motorcycle'... because that's what happened."

Write down the points you want to cover. I actually write these things out. It helps organize the flow, and it's also a process I learned from my father that works well at trial. In my example, you can see all my stars and my underlining. When you write stuff out, read it, cross things out, and rewrite it, it helps your mind absorb everything. Then, when you're presenting your summation, you have an idea of where you are on your outline, because you've gone through it. The writing-out process is essential. I do it for all my openings and all my summations.

You can see where I highlight things, and there's a flow to it. I hit strong with, "She's not admitting it to you, members of the jury." Jurors are skeptical. As a lawyer, you have to be straight with them at all stages of the trial. If a jury feels a lawyer, witness, or expert is not being straight with them, you will lose them.

Focus on credibility. It's crucial that you've established your credibility before the jury as an attorney. You backed up at trial the things you said you would prove in the opening. You've conducted yourself in such a manner that a jury will think you are a good, straightforward advocate. That follows all the way through. When you get to summation, when you're asking them to find for you, especially when you're going to ask them for money (which we'll talk about in the damages phase), your credibility is really important.

I had the ability to attack the defendant's credibility, and I came out swinging. Then to soften the blow, I said, "I'm not saying that she's a bad person. She's probably perfectly nice. What I'm saying is she's just not being straight with you." I deliver it just like that.

Look for attention-grabbing phrases. After I beat up the defendant's testimony a bit, I moved on to, "It doesn't add up." I called their theory a "phantom theory," and I used that phrase throughout my summation. I like coming up with terms like that, because a jury can grab onto them. Their theory was that somehow the plaintiff was speeding, and he lost control of his motorcycle and fell. That's what their expert said. I said, "Who do they bring in to support this phantom theory?" And I transitioned to their accident reconstruction expert witness.

I went through the questions I had asked him:

"How many times did you testify?"

"How many cases did you review for this defense firm?"

"What do you charge?"

95

I came up with $500,000 to $850,000, and I told the jury, "It's a pretty nice gig, making $50,000 to $85,000 a year from this firm. He's made over half a million dollars. Do you really think he's objective? Or do you think he's coming here to support some phantom theory? Well, let's look at what science he brought to you."

Then I attacked him. He didn't have measurements. He didn't create a diagram. My entire next section is attacking him with all the good stuff I got from him during my cross-examination (See Chapter 4 Appendix). He didn't perform a reconstruction of the collision. I asked him, "Did you even consider that maybe they collided and attempt to reconstruct that?" He said, "No, I just went with the theory that there was no collision."

Then I shifted gears to our expert. I said, "Look at this science. Look at these measurements. Look at these diagrams. This makes sense. And it's exactly what the plaintiff said." I went through the plaintiff's testimony. I introduced my expert's diagram.

Address comparative fault. In this case, I had to address the issue that there was no negligence on the plaintiff's part, because the defense will always argue comparative fault. With comparative fault, you don't want to just run from that and say, "I don't want to talk about the plaintiff's negligence." You want to address comparative fault. You want to say, "What did he do wrong?" You can say something like, "He put on his blinker, and he looked where he was going. That didn't cause this accident."

Find your style. You have to deliver your summation in a way where you're being yourself. You can't deliver a summation the way I do. And I can't deliver a summation like many other lawyers do. You can only be yourself. Whatever way you communicate, you need to share it with the jury in a way that's comfortable for you, in straightforward terms, the way you would explain it to your family, friends, or colleagues. Don't try to be a professor. Always bring the jury back to common sense, because that's what they need to apply. You have to present your case in a common-sense manner to a jury for it to be effective.

Organize your exhibits. You need to organize the exhibits that support what you want to argue to a jury, whether they are photographs, documents, or testimony. In summation, you make your argument, and then you support it with the evidence. You're taking your apples and making an apple pie to deliver to the jury.

It's vital that throughout the trial, you keep a list of all the exhibits, their numbers, and what's in evidence. You want to organize those in your outline. In my example, I circled Plaintiff's Exhibit 13. That's a photograph showing no cars in sight in the right lane. Then I pulled up Plaintiff's Exhibit 6. That's a photo that shows how far left she is. I said, "Look how much room there was to go around him."

Rewrite and review. After you've gone through your process, you can rewrite it and get your exhibits organized. Then you read through it, a lot. After you've done that, take a break, and get back and read through it again. I'll read through my outline on the morning of summation, when I wake up, to refresh myself. And by going through this process, you will be prepared when it's time to get up and deliver. It is all absorbed in your brain. You're organized, you have your evidence, you have your photos, you have your exhibits, and you know when you're going to address everything. It becomes a smoothly organized, orchestrated delivery.

Review the verdict sheet. You use the verdict sheet as another opportunity to go through your argument with the jury. In any good summation, the trial attorney will go through the verdict sheet. You'll spend a lot of time making sure that it's the proper verdict sheet for your case. And then you go through it with the jury. People ask me, "Are you allowed to? Can you do that?" Yes, you can, and yes, you should. It will be marked as a court exhibit. The court will give you a copy of it before your summation. You will stand up in front of the jury, with the verdict sheet in your hand and go through each question along with the answer you believe applies. You must do this. Because when you're done, the jury will have that verdict sheet in their deliberation room. They will look at the question and ask, "Is it yes? Is it no?" Someone will say, "What do you think this question means?" Someone else will say, "I don't think that's what that means."

So, you need to go through the verdict sheet and tell them what answers you want:

"Was the defendant negligent?"

"Yes, for all the reasons we discussed."

"Was that a substantial factor? Substantial factor means did it cause the injuries?"

97

"Of course it did."

You are giving them the answers you believe are right. You also want it to register so someone might think, "Smiley said, we should check this. I'm going with him." You hope you have a jury that's in there fighting for you.

Sample verdict sheet. Verdict sheets are all different, depending on the facts of the case. In a civil trial, you need five of six jurors to agree. In Federal Court, it must be unanimous. Here's an example of the proposed verdict sheet from Oscar's liability trial:

SUPREME COURT OF THE STATE OF NEW YORK
COUNTY OF QUEENS

X---X

OSCAR A,   Plaintiff,

-against-

CAROL R. L and PHILIP J. L,

Defendants.

X---X

VERDICT SHEET

1.Was the defendant, CAROL R. L, negligent?

At least five jurors must agree on the answer to this question.

Yes___No___

If your answer is "No," proceed no further and report to the court.

If your answer is "Yes," proceed to Question "2."

2. Was defendant, CAROL R. L's, negligence a substantial factor in causing the accident?

At least five jurors must agree on the answer to this question.

Yes___ No___

If your answer to Question "2" is "No," proceed no further and report to the court.

If your answer to Question "2" is "Yes," proceed to Question "3."

3. Was plaintiff negligent?

At least five jurors must agree on the answer to this question.

Yes___ No ___

If your answer to Question "3" is "No," proceed no further and report to the court.

If your answer to Question "3" is "Yes," proceed to Question "4."

4. Was plaintiff's negligence a substantial factor in causing the accident?

At least five jurors must agree on the answer to this question.

Yes___ No___

If your answer to Question "4" is "No," do not answer Question "5" proceed no further and report to the court.

If your answer to Question "4" is "Yes," proceed to Question "5."

5. What was the percentage of fault of the defendant and what was the percentage of fault of the plaintiff?

At least five jurors must agree on the answer to this question.

Defendant %____

Plaintiff %_____

Total must be 100%

What's great about using a verdict sheet in summation is that it gives you another opportunity to hit the highlights of your argument. You're not just saying, "Check, yes, the

99

defendant was negligent." You're going to say, "Yes, and we just discussed why. She acknowledges she hit him." And you reel off the greatest hits of your summation.

How to Address Damages

Damages are a tricky area. It's when you're talking about the value of the case. Asking a group of strangers, a jury, to award money is one of the most challenging things I've encountered in the practice of law. I still haven't figured out the best way to do it. It's always a work in progress. I'm always speaking to other lawyers and interested in how they do it. It's very tricky. Do you suggest a number? Do you not suggest a number? Do you give a range? How do you phrase it? How do you deliver it? Do you always ask for more than what you want?

First of all, you have to distinguish between hard numbers and soft numbers. Hard numbers are numbers such as an analysis that your economist came in and projected. Loss of earnings, future life care plans, past medical bills—these are all hard numbers. You can literally show these numbers to the jury. You write what you want into the verdict sheet. Sometimes you blow it up. I've seen lawyers use a big blank whiteboard and write out a number for the economic damages.

Some will even write out a number for soft numbers. Soft numbers are pain and suffering numbers. Those are numbers where there aren't any guidelines. You can't say a broken arm is worth between X and Y, and here's the proof. That's in the jury's domain, and it's very tricky. Some lawyers write those numbers out on the board and add them to the hard numbers to come up with a total. Jurors often like to see numbers because it helps them when it comes time for them to write numbers down.

Generally, when I'm switching from my liability argument in a summation that addresses damages as well, I'll transition with something simple like, "All right, now, what were the consequences of this defendant's negligence? What happened as a result of their failure to use reasonable care? We heard a lot of testimony about the damages sustained by the plaintiff."

And then you'll go through the treatment. You go through the costs, the economic numbers. Having the medical bills and anything else you can put into evidence is always good, such as income loss or future medical care. Always ask the treating physicians for any future care that they think the plaintiff may need, and ask them to testify as to the cost.

100

After laying out those hard numbers for the jury, you can say, "But that's the small part, that $1.75 million for future medical care, for wages that the plaintiff isn't going to earn, for paying past medical bills. That's a small part of this case. The real damage is the plaintiff's pain, suffering, and loss of enjoyment of life." That's where you get into, "You heard the testimony. He can't ever ride a motorcycle again, and that was his passion. What's it worth when someone takes your passion away from you forever? How do you put a number on that?"

Here's another example. "You've heard from the children in this death case about how they don't have their dad. They'll never have their father walk them down the aisle at their wedding or be there for graduation. How do you put a value on that?" Here's where you have to get creative and be persuasive. You need to have laid the foundation by making sure that your plaintiff and other witnesses gave you all the damages apples you need for your summation.

You tell a jury, "You can't unring a bell." You say, "We're all going to move on after your verdict, and we're going to live with it. I'll have other cases. My adversary will move on to other cases. The judge will have other trials. And you'll go back to your life. But for the plaintiff, your verdict will be forever. You have to think about that. Because forever is statistically another 60 years. Forever is when the plaintiff is married, hopefully with children, maybe a grandfather. You have to think about all of this. And it's my obligation as an advocate to make sure he's properly compensated."

Then it comes time to give the jury a recommendation. And there's a phrase that I learned from a prominent trial lawyer when I attended a CLE on summations many years ago. He was older, and he had a cool spiel and a Brooklyn accent. You can only be yourself. But here's what he suggested, and what I've used effectively lately:

You say, "I'm worried because if I ask you for a value for future pain and suffering, or past pain and suffering, and it's not enough money, I'm doing my client a disservice. I'm not getting my client the compensation that he deserves. But, if I ask for too much money, you may think I'm overreaching. I don't want you to think that. I don't want my credibility to take a hit, or for you to hold that against my client. So, all I can do is recommend a number. It's a number that I think is fair, and that I deliver to you the way I've delivered the trial and the evidence to you. You can

101

agree with me. If you think I'm wrong, you could give less, or you can give more. That's up to you."

I would suggest asking for a number that you think is reasonable and maybe inflated a touch, because jurors often will reduce it.

That's how I often deliver my damages request to a jury. It's not easy to do. People have their own ways, and you should do whatever works for you. If you want to give it a shot, give it a shot. But you must ask for it—you have to recommend the number. I've tried cases in other jurisdictions. In the one and only case I tried in New Jersey, right before I was preparing my summation, my local counsel said, "You're not allowed to ask for an amount of money in summation." I said, "What?! I can't ask? How do I do that?" Sometimes it's tricky.

My father once tried a case where a jury came back with more money than he asked for. That's a testament to him—you don't see that often. I haven't had the benefit of that. But I've had jurors come back with exactly the number I asked for. I tried one case where I asked for $750,000. After summations, when the jury was deliberating, the judge called me into chambers and said, "Why don't you settle the case while they're deliberating? You don't really think the jury will come back with $750,000, do you?" I said, "Probably not, but let's see what happens. Maybe they'll get close." Sure enough, the jury came back with it. It happens sometimes. But I think that was a testament to how I handled myself at the trial. And that credibility carries its way through when you ask for money.

How to Present Your Summation

When I was a younger lawyer, I'd be pacing in front of a courthouse, all dressed up, practicing and talking out loud, and another lawyer would come by and say, "You got your summation suit on kid, I see it. Go get 'em!"

People still call it your summation suit or your summation outfit. You want to dress nicely like you do for openings. Get all the stuff out of your pockets. Don't hold a pen or a pad in your hands. Don't read from your notes. You don't need to read from your outline if you have prepared properly.

Ask for a few minutes. When you get to the courtroom, if you need a little time, you can ask the judge, "Your Honor, can I have five minutes to organize the courtroom?" You can line all of your exhibits up against the rail where the jury is facing you, so you see them all. It becomes an orchestrated, smooth process. You want to be buttoned up, with no distractions.

Keep your notes nearby. Have your pad or outline on a counsel table, lectern, or podium off to the side. Then you can pause, walk over, do the water trick where you take a sip of water, look down at your pad, flip a couple of pages so you know where you're going next, and get back up and engage. These outlines are your safety net, so you don't go blank. You have it there as a guide if you need it.

So many times, I will see a lawyer get up with the pad in one hand and a pen in another and say, "Hey, members of the jury, here's what we've learned." They're looking at their pad and checking things off with their pen. I despise that. I think when you lose eye contact, you lose a jury. Even when I give CLE presentations, I try to look at everyone. I'm not reading with my head down, although I have my outline if I need it.

Find the best place to stand. You want to stand in the well, which is the area in front of the jury box. Don't stay behind the lectern or a podium. Almost every judge will let you stand in the well. If they make you stay at the lectern, move to the side slightly. Talk with your hands if that's your style. I like to be demonstrative. I don't think there's anything wrong with that. But be you—if you don't want to move your hands, hold them together in front of you or behind you, or keep them at your sides.

Engage with the jury. Engaging with the jury is key to delivering a good summation (and opening, for that matter). Talk to and with the jury. Scroll the jury, nod, and pause. Make brief eye contact with each of the jury members at some point. But don't get too close to them or invade their personal space. You don't want to get right up to them or look at a particular juror too hard or too long.

Pause and change your inflection. After you say something like, "She wasn't being straight with you, members of the jury," pause for a second. Let the good stuff sink in. Put up your exhibits and deliver everything nicely and smoothly.

Finish strong. When you're wrapping up, you want to finish strong like you did in your opening. Don't just say "Thank you" and walk off thinking, "Thank God, I got that done." Finish by saying something like, "'I hit a motorcycle.' That's what happened here, members of the jury. I know with your common sense, applied to the evidence, that you'll do the right thing when it's time to deliberate in the jury room."

Then say, "On behalf of my client," say your client's name, and your client should nod as you've instructed, "and myself, I'd like to thank you for the time and attention you've given to this case, and the time and attention you will continue to give this case in your deliberations. Thank you so much." You smile, you pause, you walk strong, and you go and sit down. That's how you finish a summation. It worked for me in Oscar's case—I won a 100% liability verdict against the defendants.

Luck is always a factor. You always need some luck. No matter how I prepare, I don't always win my cases, and I don't always get 100%. But if you've prepared, you've put your heart into your summation, you've summarized everything, and you've put in the effort, that's all you can do. Then it's in the jury's hands. You may get a great result with one group of jurors, and with the same exact trial and the same exact summation, you could get a different result with different jurors. I've lost a case or two. And when I speak with jurors after, they say things like, "Mr. Smiley, you're great. You didn't even look at your notes, and you were very persuasive, but we found for the other side."

Ultimately, you want to win. But all you can do is feel good about the effort you've put in. As long as you've prepared and delivered, you've done your job. That's the key to delivering a successful summation.

Summation Example

Also annexed to this chapter, as Appendix-2, is my closing argument from a liability-only case I tried years ago in Brooklyn. My client, Nell, was exercising with a personal trainer at a well-known gym chain. The trainer had her perform a "toe tap" exercise where she stood at a weightlifting bench and tapped one toe on the bench, then brought it down to the floor, then tapped the other toe on the bench and brought it down to the floor. She caught her toe on the bench, fell backwards, and broke both her wrists.

My adversary said it was all her fault and there was an inherent risk to training. You can see in my summation that I talk in common sense. I said, "Members of the jury, does that make sense to you? Come on. You're from Brooklyn. That doesn't make sense." It's OK to talk like that. I was successful—I won a 100% liability verdict against the gym and trainer.

CHAPTER 5 APPENDIX-1

MY CLOSING ARGUMENT OUTLINE FROM OSCAR'S CASE

CHAPTER 5 APPENDIX-2

MY CLOSING ARGUMENT IN NELL'S CASE

```
1        MR. SMILEY:  Thank you, your Honor.  May it

2    please the Court, Judge ███, counsel, members of the

3    jury, hello.  This case is brought against ███████,

4    the company C███, as a result of the negligence of

5    its employee, Gavin ████.  The judge will instruct

6    you that the gym is responsible for his acts.  ███████,

7    big gym chain.  We have heard, at least during this

8    trial, that they have twelve franchises or gyms on

9    the east coast alone, over 200 trainers, all that are

10   employed in the industry.

11        We bring this case against ███████, and isn't

12   it so interesting that ██████ didn't bring one person

13   in here to sit on that stand before you, members of

14   the jury, to vouch for their trainer?  You didn't

15   hear from one person from ██████ come in here and

16   say, yeah, if he was our trainer, we stand behind

17   him, he was trained properly, he followed proper

18   procedures, he picked proper exercises, he spotted

19   properly.  Not one to vouch.  Interesting.

20        Now, we had Mr. C███, you may recall William

21   C███, we called him to the stand to testify.  I

22   tried to ask him as much as I could about ██████, the

23   practices and policies.  We learned a little bit

24   about forms that have to be documented.  When I got
```

1   into the area of spotting and toe-tapping, and all of

2   that, objection--

3   MR. ███████ : Objection.

4   MR. SMILEY: Objection. Objection, when I

5   went to ask him all that, objection, objection.

6   MR. ███████ : Objection. May we approach?

7   THE COURT: No. Overruled.

8   MR. SMILEY: And then after I was done asking

9   the best I could, so you jurors can decide this case

10   on the issues and the facts and have the proper

11   information, it was then Mr. ███████ 's opportunity.

12   He had William ███ on the stand. Mr. ███ , who we

13   learned was the head of personal training for the

14   entire east coast of ███████ gym, he personally

15   oversaw personal training of all twelve gyms, all the

16   ones in New York City, the one involved in Nell's

17   accident in Brooklyn. He was in charge of over 200

18   personal trainers, the training program, the personal

19   training managers. He was sitting right here for

20   you, members of the jury.

21   And when it was time for the defense to ask

22   him a question to vouch for his trainer --

23   MR. ███████ : Objection.

24   MR. SMILEY: --did you hear one question

25   being asked?

1   MR. █████: Your Honor, may we approach?

2   THE COURT: Overruled. No.

3   MR. SMILEY: No, you didn't. Ask yourselves

4   why. Why not? Not only did they not ask Mr. C██ a

5   question to vouch for their employee to say what the

6   standards were or anything like that, but they could

7   have brought an expert witness in here to testify

8   before you, members of the jury.

9   MR. █████: Objection, your Honor.

10   THE COURT: Overruled.

11   MR. SMILEY: They could have brought an expert

12   the same way we did. They didn't have to. But, they

13   could have. Certainly, they could find an expert

14   either within their own ranks, one of their 200 plus

15   trainers or someone within the industry. It's

16   █████. Certainly, they could reach out to someone

17   in the sports and fitness industry with credentials

18   like Mr. Nelson to come sit in this chair, take an

19   oath to tell you folks the truth and tell you about

20   proper standards and to vouch for the actions of

21   Gavin █████ to tell you, yeah, it's okay that he had

22   Nell do that toe-tap exercise, even though it was

23   over twelve inches high with a bench and she'd never

24   done it before, yeah, that was fine, yeah, he

25   followed all the rules, it was okay, he didn't have
1   to break her fall or prevent her fall or be her

2   safety net.

3   Not one person. Ask yourselves why not. You

4   know why not. You know exactly why not. As you sit

5   here, come on, you're from Brooklyn, you know why

6   because if somebody could come in here and say

7   that under oath on the witness stand to lay their

8   credentials on the line for you to say, yes, I'm an

9   expert, I have been in this industry, I know the

10   standards, I know how it works, he did everything

11   right. If there was one person who could do that,

12   maybe we would have heard that, but we didn't.

13   That's because nobody could come to vouch for what he

14   did, that's why, because he was negligent. That's

15   why, members of the jury.

16   The only person we heard from from the

17   defense case was Gavin, the trainer, himself who was

18   responsible for this occurrence and accident. I'll

19   submit to you he's probably not the most objective

20   person to hear from about the standards and we didn't

21   even hear that from him. He wasn't asked what the

22   standards were at ████, how he was trained, what he

23   was taught to do. We didn't hear any of that. His

24   lawyer could have asked him. His lawyer could have

25   brought out his credentials, his experience, his

1   training.

2   Was he even asked what certifications, where
3
4   he went to school, what kind of training they give

5   him at Crunch, what experience or expertise, what

6   qualifications he had to make sure Nell was trained

7   properly? Nell didn't pick him out of a website or

8   go to him in his own gym. She went to ███.

9   You heard from her she had an expectation

10   that ███'s trainers were qualified and knew what

11   they were doing and she could be safe. We didn't

12   hear any-- we don't know anything about that man.

13   Certainly, we know he wasn't an expert. Could have

14   gone through the same thing we did with Mr. Nelson,

15   laid out his credentials here and asked Judge ███ to

16   recognize him in the field of personal training.

17   That wasn't done.

18   So, what did we learn from Gavin? What

19   pieces of information that are important for you

20   folks to know in your deliberations in this case?

21   Well, a few standard rules we did know about. We

22   know he didn't follow -- he didn't fill out the PARKU

23   (ph.) or the fitness assessment or the goal

24   assessment forms. These things are important.

25   The defense may try to minimize it and say it

26   didn't matter, it's part of the process of trying to

1   get to know the client and part of the process of

2   getting to train the clients. He didn't do any of

3   that. He put her right to it, got right to work.

4   And we know that on just the second day of training,

5   the day that Nell told him she was sore, it was a

6   different experience for her.

7   We know that he decided for whatever reason

8   to pick this exercise out of a hat, this toe-tap

9   exercise. And he told us, oh, she could do it, she

10   did jumping-jacks, might as well have her do this.

11   Didn't give you any explanation, any actual logic or

12   reasoning for his training or experience to explain

13   why he would choose an exercise like that for a woman

14   like Nell. She wasn't there to train as a

15   professional athlete. She wasn't training for a

16   marathon or anything like that. She just wanted to get

17   fit.

18   So, he picks this exercise out of thin air.

19   He claims to have done a program progress and laid it

20   all out. You think he did it? That's up to you. We

21   didn't hear about it. We didn't see it. We didn't

22   know it existed and he picks this exercise for her to

23   do, knowing she's never done it before. That's

24   important, ladies and gentlemen, it's an exercise she

25   hadn't done before. It doesn't matter what her

1   ability was, it doesn't matter if she could do it

2   like a shining star athlete, doesn't matter if I

3   could do it, if Mr. ████ could do it, none of that

4   matters.

5   Matters what her background was. Nell had

6   trained with Telly ████, we heard, forty-eight

7   times. Defense wants you to believe because she

8   trained with her, that makes her an expert athlete.

9   What we know is she went with a trainer. She put her

10   trust in great experience, working safely, did her

11   exercises that she felt confident in doing and that

12   her trainer was there for her to establish that

13   trust. That's all we know.

14   And what we do know is that she had never

15   done a toe-tap before. For whatever reason, Telly

16   didn't have her do it, not at an elevation, not even

17   on the ground, she had never done it before. Gavin

18   knew that. Knowing she had never done it, she didn't

19   even do it just on the floor, just to get the

20   movement down or holding a ball or anything like

21   this, he brought her over to a high bench to do it.

22   He demonstrates it and he tells her to do it, knowing

23   she had never done it before, okay?

24   It's not bad enough that he picks it in the

25   first place, but then, knowing she's never done it

1   before, he's supposed to be there for her at the very

2   least, let her know, Nell, listen, you may stumble,

3   you may fall, this could happen, I'm here for you,

4   I'm going to catch you, I'm right here, you get here,

5   do the exercise, I'm right here for you, I'll grab

6   you, I'll step in, I'll be there for you.

7   He purposefully didn't tell her any risks, he

8   didn't tell her she could fall, he didn't tell her

9   how to fall, he didn't tell her, I'll be there, I

10 gotcha, knowing she never done it. He stands there,

11 says, go for it, give me twenty. He could have held

12 her hand, said, let's try the movement, let's do it

13 on a floor, let's do it at a lower progress, all

14 these things he didn't do.

15 And then, members of the jury, when it's time

16 for her to do it, proper standard of care, according

17 to Delon Nelson, is to be there, be on it, have a

18 hand, be ready 'cause you don't know what's going to

19 happen, you don't know if she's going to be able to

20 do it or not. You just don't know. And knowing what

21 Gavin admitted on the stand, that she could fall

22 backwards, he's there, he's watching her feet, he's

23 ready, and sure enough, that's what happened. She

24 couldn't do it right. Okay.

25   She never done the exercise before. I don't

1   know if anybody in this room could have done it.

2   Right? If we all could have, some could, some

3   couldn't. She couldn't. She tried and she failed.

4   He set her up for failure. He gave her something

5   difficult and challenging she had never done, wasn't

6   there to aid her, hold her hand, make sure she could

7   do it right, learn the moves right.

8   And then, even though he claims to have been

9   here, he's standing there, sure enough, she falls and

10   she falls backwards. She doesn't fall that way. She

11   doesn't fall in some unusual way. His testimony was,
12

13   oh, it was unexpected. It wasn't unexpected. This

14   is exactly what he knew could happen, that she could

15   fall. I still don't get his explanation. I don't

16   think anybody could, that she stepped up and she

17   jumped up and jumped back like a Jackie Chan move or

18   some catwoman thing where she does a somersault. You

19   can't even get a hand on it.

20   It just doesn't make sense. It defies logic,

21   defies common sense, if he's doing his job, he's

22   right here for her. You heard him say, he's fit,

23   works out regularly, he's a trainer, he's got fast

24   reflexes. Actually, what you'd expect a trainer to

25   be. He isn't some guy off the street who's never

26   been in a gym before. He's supposed to be in shape

1   and know what to do. It's his job. He's right here.

2   And the very first move, she stumbles back,

3   he doesn't step in, he doesn't grab her, he reach for

4   her. Does that make any sense? Not only does he not

5   catch her, which by the way, he said, oh, it's not my

6   job to catch my client if she falls during an

7   exercise, it's not my job. You think if he told Nell

8   that before she started working out with him, she'd

9   still want to train with this man? Not my job and

10   she falls back, and he didn't get a hand on her,

11   okay, think about that. Just think about that.

12   He's standing here. She falls backwards. He

13   doesn't say, well, listen, I grabbed her, we both

14   tumbled to the ground, I got my hand on her wrist,

15   she fell, it was kind of awkward, I tried to break

16   her fall, she went this way, I went that way.

17   Nothing. Nothing. He didn't get any part of her

18   body. He didn't touch her arm, didn't touch her leg,

19   her hip. Nothing. Use your common sense. Come on.

20   And if you use your common sense, it will

21   tell you that anybody standing there doing their job

22   would have gotten a hand on her. He wasn't there,

23   okay? He wasn't there. He was standing off to the

24   side. He said, go, give it, give me twenty and she

25   took a header straight back. And the only thing that

1   broke Nell's fall was her wrists. That's it.

2   You heard the ground broke her fall. Not
3   Gavin. That was his job. That's what the evidence
4
5   showed. There's no dispute about that, members of
6
7   the jury. And we heard about that from Delon Nelson,

8   an expert who took the stand here and testified he

8   laid his credentials on the line. He took an oath to

9   tell you the truth.

10   And what he said just makes sense. I mean,

11   he's been in this industry, look at his credentials.

12   He has a bachelor's degree in Physical Education and

13   health science. He taught at City College, then he

14   went out as a trainer at ████, of all places, for

15   six years. He was promoted to personal training

16   manager, position higher than Gavin has, someone who

17   oversees the trainers. He told you for a while he's

18   at a popular ████ in Manhattan.

19   He was the liaison with publications with the

20   media to talk about fitness. He was the head trainer

21   selected to work with Ms. USA pageant. He worked

22   there. He knew his stuff. He had certification

23   after certification. He trained kick-boxers. He

24   kick-boxed. He went to Thailand. He's been around

25   for seventeen years, training thousands of people.

26   Okay. I think that's some good experience.

1   Certainly, a lot more than anything else you heard.

2   What he said makes sense. Let's listen to

3   what Delon Nelson said. First of all, he said that

4   people come to a gym and they hire a trainer for

5   their safety. That's the-- number one, of course,

6   you hire a trainer to get you fit and get in shape,

7   you want to be safe, you don't want to hurt yourself,

8   you don't want to be one of those people who shows up

9   to a gym and starts piling weights on a rack and does

10   something and gets injured. You want to be safe.

11   That's the trainer's job, to pick proper

12   exercises and to make sure your client doesn't get

13   injured while doing them. That makes sense. When I

14   asked him about the toe-tap exercise, he

15   demonstrated, came down here and he showed you how to

16   do it on the floor first and how a client can get

17   exercise out of that.

18   And then he said if that's not enough just on

19   the floor, give the client a physio ball, that makes

20   it harder. And if that's too easy, let her raise it

21   above her head. There's no risk of training or fall

22   or getting injured on an apparatus. He doesn't

23   consider any of that. Then you can increase the

24   ball, you can increase the rate. And then if all

25   that fails, then you can start with a low elevation.

1   I went over to the step over here by the witness

2   stand. He said, you can do six inches, you can do

3   the exercise on six inches. No reason to go all the

4   way up over a foot high on the bench for the very

5   first time.

6   Not only did he say it as an expert with his

7   education and experience in the field, but it also

8   just makes sense. It just makes sense. He said that

9   beginner level, this exercise would be at no

10   elevation or up to six inches. Intermediate level of

11   this exercise would be six inches to twelve inches.

12   And over twelve inches would be advanced. Mr. Nelson

13   said the only reason he picked that exercise to have

14   one of his clients do would be one of his Muay Tai

15   kickboxing clients because those are athletes that

16   need to be in crazy condition shape to go into a ring

17   and fight for their job. It wasn't Nell.

18   There's no need to do it. No need to have

19   her go right to that. You've got to crawl before you

20   can walk, before you can run, before you can jump.
21
22   He didn't get in an explanation for it. Gavin didn't

23   give a proper explanation and nobody from Crunch came

24   in to say it was appropriate to advance her right to

25   that.

26   Delon explained-- Delon Nelson said, our job

1   as trainer is to give a safety net. He gave a great

2   analogy. I want you to consider the trapeze analogy,

3   if a client is going to go and swing from a trapeze

4   and a client sees there's a net under there and sees

5   somebody go first and swings and goes flying off,

6   they don't catch-- they don't do the proper move, the

7   net catches them, they bounce down, the client knows

8   the net is there, says, okay, I'm going to give this

9   a shot, looks kind of hard, kind of difficult, I know

10   if I don't do it right, the net will catch me.

11   That's the trainer's job, to be that safety net.

12   Then imagine going up on that trapeze,

13   thinking the net's there, swinging and stumbling and

14   falling off, falling down, and there's no net. You

15   go crashing to the ground. That's what happened in

16   this case, members of the jury, Gavin ██ was

17   supposed to be Nell's safety net and wasn't there for

18   her. That's what happened. That was his job.

19   That's what the evidence showed. And there's been no

20   dispute about it, frankly, no dispute, whatsoever.

21   Gavin failed. Now he set her up for failure.

22   He picked an exercise that was too advanced. And

23   knowing she had never done it before, he should have

24   been there and ready for her. He should have helped

25   her. He should have progressed her. He should have

1   caught her, prevented her from falling, gotten his

2   hands on her.

3   Members of the jury, we heard from Nell.

4   Now, it's interesting that the defense wants you to

5   think that Nell is negligent, Nell did something

6   negligent. She did the exercise wrong. That's

7   negligence? Haven't we all been in situations where

8   we've been asked to try something and you try and you

9   just don't do it right? Does that make her

10   negligent? If anything, if you look at what Nell had

11   to say about her experience and her background in

12   selecting a trainer, everything was quite reasonable,

13
14   to say the least.

15   At the time, she was thirty-seven, bartender,

16   she just wanted to get in shape. She wanted to lose

17   a little bit of weight, feel good about herself and

18   get a little bit fit. And she decided to do it by

19   hiring a trainer. She paid for that safety net. She

20   didn't go off half-cocked into the gym and say, let

21   me mess around and try to get myself in shape.

22   When you hear about waivers and you know the

23   risks and when you sign that form to join the gym

24   with all the fine print in it, saying you don't know

25   the risks of injury in the gym. That's not this

26   case. We're not here saying if someone gets injured

1   while working out, they have a lawsuit, there's

2   negligence. People get injured all sorts of ways,

3   but not like this. Nell wasn't there messing around.

4   She wasn't trying to do something.

5   She didn't say, oh, I'm going to try this

6   exercise, I saw somebody do it on You Tube or TV, I'm

7   going to see if I can do it. She didn't do it.

8   She's not negligent. If anything, she was

9   reasonable. On a bartender's salary, she budgeted to

10   have a trainer and she told you she went to the gym,

11   if it wasn't for yoga, to work with a trainer to

12   guide her through and work great with. That's what

13   she had Gavin for when he asked her to do this

14   exercise.

15   Oh, she's negligent. The defense will have

16   you believe she should have said, oh, by the way, I'm

17   not going to do that exercise, oh, you better get

18   here close to me. She's negligent for not doing

19   that. She put her trust in him. She was reasonable.

20   Given her experience with Telly, it's her

21   understanding you trust your trainer. Trainer says

22   you can do it, say okay, it looks a little scarier,

23   but I'll try it, knowing that the trainer's the

24   safety net and there if you mess up.

25   That's reasonableness. That's not

1   negligence. Nell explained her reasoning. She said,

2   I was tired, my legs were sore, he demonstrated,

3   looked hard, I said, really? He said, yeah. I said,

4   okay, I'll give it a try. She was trying her best.

5   It wasn't negligent. Think about that, members of

6   the jury. He was a safety net. He failed her.

7   She didn't do anything wrong in this case.

8   The fact that she had been to a gym before or was

9   there during the month of January, she explained she

10   went for yoga, the month of January, she went to meet

11   with the advisor to find out about switching her

12   trainers. What did she do wrong here? She didn't

13   do anything wrong.

14   Now, the verdict sheet that you're going to

15   get, I'm going to go through it, each question. The

16   first question that you'll have is, were the

17   defendants negligent? Yes or no. That's a decision

18   that five out of six of you will have to make, yes or

19   no. The answer to this-- there's really only one

20   answer when you look at the real evidence that you

21   heard is yes.

22   We heard from Delon Nelson, the only expert

23   testimony, you heard in this case that it is a

24   departure from good and accepted training practice to

25   have a client with any level ability do an exercise

1   like this, toe-tap like 12.4 inches high without

2   first making sure she can do the movement at a lower

3   level first and properly do the exercise, that's

4   negligence. That's what you heard from the evidence.

5   That means you check off yes.

6   The other negligence is the failure to be

7   there to spot her, so that if she did fail in trying,

8   that you can catch her, prevent the fall. That was

9   negligence. And we don't have to prove both. We

10   only have to prove one. But, I feel we have clearly

11   proven both. And you can pick one or both, either or

12   all the above, any way or shape, he was negligent and

13   there was no evidence to the contrary.

14   After you check yes to the negligence part,

15   the next one is: Was the defendant's negligence a

16   substantial factor in causing the incident. The

17   judge is going to instruct you on what that means,

18   but basically, did it cause it, did his negligence

19   cause her accident? The answer's yes. Again, check

20   it. He shouldn't have had her doing the exercise.

21   That was a substantial factor. He should have

22   prevented her fall. That was a substantial factor.

23   The answer's yes.

24   The question after that is: Was the

25   plaintiff negligent? Now, the judge will instruct

1   you when you get to this part, the burden shifts just

2   the same way. We have the burden to prove that the

3   defendant, through Gavin, was negligent. The burden

4   shifts to the defense.

5   MR. ██████: Objection.

6   THE COURT: Sustained.

7   MR. SMILEY: And it's up to them to prove to

8   you --

9   MR. KLAUBER: Objection, your Honor. He's

10   continuing with the same --

11   THE COURT: No.

12   MR. ██████: It's up to them.

13   MR. SMILEY: It's up to them to prove to you

14   that she was negligent, just like some evidence for

15   you to think there was some credible evidence here

16   that she did something that wasn't reasonable. There

17   is none. If you collectively, amongst yourself,

18   think about this trial, there's nothing that says

19   she's negligent. The answer's no, not even a piece

20   of evidence to consider about.

21   And then you don't even get to the remainder,

22   which would be if her negligence was a substantial

23   factor, you don't even get to that question, which

24   would be no 'cause there was no negligence.

25   Last question that's here that if you did

1   find that the defendant was negligent and Nell was

2   negligent, then you're asked to divide up the pie to

3   100 percent, okay? That's how the verdict works.

4   And you all have this when you go to the jury room.

5   Members of the jury, the evidence was clear

6   here. Okay. And again, you've got to remember that

7   it's not about who can and who can't do this

8   exercise. Mr. ███████ wants you to think he can do

9   the exercise and it's simple. That wasn't the case.

10   He wasn't even sure. Even assuming he's the best

11   athlete in the world, he's in great shape, he can do

12   this exercise, that doesn't mean it's right for Nell.

13   Doesn't mean a thing.

14   You heard the example Delon Nelson gave to

15   you, if he asked everybody in this room to do

16   push-ups, some would be able to do it great, some

17   would be on their knees, some, one arm, everybody

18   different levels. You have to know and you have to

19   progress. Okay.

20   There's no doubt about the negligence. And

21   if there is, this is what I ask of you, members of

22   the jury, when you go into that jury room after her

23   Honor instructs you and you're deliberating, if

24   there's any doubt in any of your minds as to whether

25   or not the answer's yes, consider two questions.

1   And I'm not going to tell you the answer, I'm

2   going to ask among yourselves, question number one:

3   If Gavin ████ was really following the proper

4   standards of care in his profession in the industry

5   of personal training, in selecting Nell, given

6   everything he knew and didn't know about her, given

7   these accidents, if it was proper, how come not one

8   person took an oath to vouch for him? That's

9   question number one.

10   Question number two, if he was really there,

11   if he was really where he claims to be, if he was

12   really where he was supposed to be, spotting her on

13   this exercise, how come he didn't get a hand on her?

14   Forget about catching her, ready to fall, how come he

15   didn't get a hand on her?

16   On behalf of myself and on behalf of Nell,

17   you've been extremely patient. I appreciate that.

18   So does she. Very important matters to everybody

19   involved in this action. And I thank you for your

20   patience. I thank you for your attention that you've

21   given to this case and continue to give. Thank you.

EPILOGUE

IMPROVE YOUR SKILLS

To have true success in the law, you must keep learning and improving your skills.

Keep going to court. Keep trying cases. Keep reading. Keep learning. Always keep an open mind.

Seek out other attorneys for guidance and collaboration.

Refer back to the chapters of this book as you prepare for each trial.

If you would like to learn more from me, I have a podcast called "The Mentor Esq." which can be found on all major podcast platforms. Videos and course materials from my monthly continuing legal education (CLE) lectures on behalf of The New York State Academy of Trial Lawyers can be found at www.TheMentorEsq.com.

To learn more about my law firm, Smiley & Smiley, LLP, please visit www.SmileyLaw.com. We welcome referrals from other attorneys on matters involving serious personal injury, wrongful death, medical malpractice, and insurance coverage litigation.

You can follow me on Instagram @TheMentorEsq.

I would love to hear from you. I pride myself on always being available to assist other lawyers. I offer complimentary thirty-minute Zoom sessions. If you would like to connect, please email me at asmiley@smileylaw.com. I promise to respond, usually within 24 hours.

AUTHOR'S NOTE

This book would not be possible without the mentoring of my father, Guy I. Smiley, Esq., and support from Jason D. Friedman, Esq., Michael S. Solomon, Esq., Rosa M. Feeney, Esq. and my Smiley Law family: Madlyn Solivan, Islande Maitre and Jacqueline Valentin. Thank you all for your loyalty and friendship.

I also owe a great debt of gratitude to Brian Cristiano, my friend, business coach, marketing genius, confidant, and motivator. Special thanks to my editor Stephanie Thurrott and to Tim Lord and his marketing team at Boston Impressions for creating the cover art for launching the Mentor Esq. Handbook Series.

Finally, everything I do in life is on behalf of, and from the support of, my wife, Paula, and my daughter, Elle. Thank you both for putting up with me and for your unconditional love and encouragement. I love you.

Made in the USA
Columbia, SC
03 December 2024

48368511R00155